The Last Lap

The Emergence of the One New Man

The
Last
Lap

The Emergence of
the One New Man

Sid Roth

The Last Lap: The Emergence of the One New Man
ISBN #0-910267-03-0
©2001 by Sid Roth, Messianic Vision

PUBLISHED BY
M V Press
P.O. Box 1918
Brunswick, GA 31521

COVER DESIGN BY
Now You See It! graphics

EDITED BY
Robert C. DuVall

Printed in the United States of America

To my daughter Leigh and son-in-law Greg Williamson

Leigh is Jewish and Greg is a Gentile. Their first daughter is named Olivia because she is the fruit of the Jew and Gentile grafted into the Olive tree.

Contents

Foreword

Imet Sid Roth at a service in Jacksonville, Florida where my wife, Kathy, and I were ministering. Sid was so hungry for a touch from God that he shook under the power of the Holy Spirit. As I've watched Sid over the years, I've seen his passion for the deeper things of the Lord increase the mantle to bring a fresh move of God into the Jewish community. Many of Sid's insights in this book bridge the great chasm between the church and the Jewish people. As the bridge is built bringing the Jewish and non-Jewish church together, we are prepared to take the next step in fulfilling God's purposes in this last hour.

Although the Jewish people are important to what God is doing in the earth, they have suffered greatly from anti-Semitism promulgated by some of the early church leaders. This book reveals the roots of anti-Semitism in the church and prophetically proclaims an outline for the next great move of God.

I agree wholeheartedly with Sid that the church is incomplete without Jewish believers coming together with non-Jewish believers as they did in the book of Acts. Most Christians don't realize that the first apostles and leaders were Jews who evangelized the non-Jewish world. Now is the time for Gentiles to return the favor by letting the glory of God flow through us back to the Jewish people.

This book is part of something I have longed for and dreamed of for many years—to see Jewish apostles and prophets again walking the earth. As these Jewish leaders are raised up and released, we will see the end-time church become "One New Man," manifesting the glory of God. Ephesians 4:4-6 states:

> "We are all one body, we have the same Spirit, and we have all been called to the same glorious future. There is only one Lord, one faith, one baptism, and there is only one God and Father, who is over us all and in us all and living through us all" (NLT).

Messiah Jesus "has broken down the middle wall of division between [Jew and Gentile]" (Ephesians 2:14).

When the two come together creating One New Man, the glory will increase with healings, miracles, and the greatest harvest of souls in history.

Steve Gray
World Revival Church
Kansas City, Missouri

Introduction

The establishment of God's kingdom on earth is like a relay race. One man runs a lap and passes the baton to the next team member. The strongest runner runs the last lap.

Adam started the race but fell and didn't complete his lap. Abraham and his children (the Jewish people) then picked up the baton and ran the laps faithfully. But 2,000 years ago, we Jewish people got very, very tired.

So we passed the baton to the Gentile Christians. After centuries of running with the Gospel, they too are beginning to wear down. It's the last lap. And it doesn't look like our team is going to win.

Should the Gentile Christians pass the baton to the Messianic Jews (Jewish believers in Jesus)? No, they are stronger than ever, but not strong enough.

What then should the church do? A champion is needed if we are to win the race.

Wait.... I see who is going to get the baton. It's not the Messianic Jews. It's not the Gentile Christians. It is Jewish *and* Gentile believers, holding the baton together.

Now I don't see two any more. I see One New Man. The two have been made one in Jesus. He is the Second Adam. He is our champion. We win!

1

When the Pattern is Right...

I am a Jew. Although I attended a traditional synagogue as I was growing up, it never dawned on me that I could know God. The stories about Moses, Noah, and Abraham belonged to another era. God seemed to be a million miles away—not relevant to my life. Even the older men in the synagogue, who appeared to be the most devout, were more interested in the ritualistic prayers and fellowship with their friends than intimacy with God.

Today, most Jewish people are more secular than religious. When I was young, Jews at least went to the synagogue on high holidays like Rosh Hoshanah and Yom Kippur. Now the majority of my people do not attend services at all.

The Last Lap

When I encountered Jesus at the age of thirty, everything in my world changed. I not only knew God was real, but I now knew Him personally by experience. My biggest shock was to discover that Christians, on the whole, act like most Jews. They know about God. They believe in Him. They think they will probably go to heaven. Yet some have greater intimacy with their denomination than with God. Others attend church merely for the social interaction. These Sunday and "high holiday" (Easter and Christmas) Christians compartmentalize God to their convenience. They treat Jesus more as servant than Lord. They surrender Sunday mornings—not their lives.

Many churches have evolved into nothing more than human warehouses. Members are made to feel as if they are acceptable to God without repentance of sin. Their church experience is as professional spectators who never fulfill their destinies in God. Tragically, many do not even have a personal relationship with Jesus.

Over the years I began to see that even some of the better churches are filled with religious tradition. The pastors appear to be more concerned with including the offering, announcements, and a full sermon (and ending on time) rather than yielding to the leading of the Holy Spirit.

The more I hungered for greater intimacy with God, the more dissatisfied I became. Then God led me into a study of the history of the early church. The blinders of tradition fell from my eyes. I began to see the Scriptures in a whole new light.

Now I understand why there are so few miracles, even in believing, Spirit-filled churches. Now I know why there is so little compassion for the souls of men and for the poor. Now I know why the same sins of secular society pervade the church. Now I know how we have grieved the Holy Spirit through ignorance, compromise, tradition, and the fear of man. Now I know why the glory under Moses was greater than our best churches today. The answer is the message of this book.

God has been waiting for a generation of believers to follow the cloud of His presence just as the Israelites followed the cloud in the wilderness. The cloud is moving. Will you follow the cloud to glory or will you remain stuck in your old ways?

Only a few of the older believers will enter this new land. The rest will observe it from afar. I'm hungry for more. What about you?

Just as God had a specific plan for the Israelites to enter the promised land, He instructed them on how to enter His glory. God said to Moses, "See that you make all things according to the **pattern...**"

(Hebrews 8:5). The pattern is God's bridge to intimacy. When the pattern is right, the glory explodes.

Notice I did not say "formula," but "pattern." Man wants to place God in a box. This is why we have so many religions and denominations. God is too big to be limited by our attempts to define Him. We cannot reduce His pattern to a formula.

That is what many did with a popular teaching about standing on God's Word for healing. Although there is great truth in that teaching, sometimes the healing did not manifest. Those who knew God by the formula were quickly offended and abandoned their belief in healing. Some lost their faith in God altogether. But those who had genuine faith in God used that disappointment to draw closer to Him. The biblical pattern always leads to greater intimacy with God.

It also leads to unity between Jew and Gentile. I believe that today God is calling us to a new level in which both Jewish and Gentile believers will come together as One New Man—yielded to His Spirit and walking in power.

"For I am about to do a brand-new thing. See, I have already begun!" (Isaiah 43:19a, NLT).

First the Natural, Then the Spiritual
God's pattern that defines the relationship between the church and the Jewish people is explained in

1 Corinthians 15:46: "The spiritual is not first, but the natural, and afterward the spiritual." First, God acts with His natural "witness" people, Israel, then He acts with His spiritual people, the church. His true church is made up of those who genuinely believe in Jesus as Savior and Lord. The church and Israel are "mishpochah," Hebrew for "family." Whatever happens to Israel dramatically affects the restoration of the church.

For example, in 1897 Theodore Herzl convened the first Zionist Congress in Basel, Switzerland to investigate the formation of a Jewish homeland. The beginning of the restoration of the Land was followed by the beginning of the restoration of the manifest presence of the Holy Spirit back to the church. On New Year's Eve 1900, at a Bible school in Topeka, Kansas, a 30-year-old student named Agnes Ozman began to speak in tongues—the start of the Pentecostal Revival. Several days later, Charles Parham and other students also received the baptism of the Holy Spirit with the gift of speaking in tongues. After William Seymour sat under Parham's teaching, he took this fire to a home prayer meeting in Los Angeles that birthed the world famous Azusa Street Revival.

Around the time when Israel became a nation in 1948, God responded by bringing the healing revival to the United States. Over 100 evangelists like Oral Roberts, Kathryn Kuhlman, T. L. Osborn, and Kenneth Hagin began tremendous healing ministries. Billy Graham's ministry started then also.

In 1967 Israel regained possession of Jerusalem for the first time since the temple was destroyed. That same year the Catholic Charismatic movement started. It went on to impact Christians from all denominations. The late 1960s also gave birth to the "Jesus Movement" by which thousands of hippies were swept into the Kingdom.

Around the time of the Yom Kippur War in 1973, there was a revival among Jewish people resulting in the modern-day Messianic Jewish movement.

Even Israel's supposed peace agreements affect the church. Israel signed an agreement with Jordan in 1994 and with the Palestine Liberation Organization (PLO) the following year. About the same time, revival exploded at the Toronto Airport Church in Canada and the Holy Trinity Brompton Church in England.

What's Next?

Do you want to know what will be the next move of God on the church? Watch Israel! Because of sin, God scattered the Jewish people to the four corners of the earth. But in the last days He promises to restore them back to Israel (Ezekiel 37:21).

When the Pattern is Right...

In the Old Covenant, the nation of Israel was a "divided" land. The Northern Kingdom was called "Israel" and the Southern Kingdom, "Judah." Judah and Israel fought with each other. God promises to restore these two Kingdoms and return them to their land. They will be "one" nation under one King:

> "And I will make them one nation in the land, on the mountains of Israel; and one king shall be king over them all; they shall no longer be two nations, nor shall they ever be divided into two kingdoms again" (Ezekiel 37:22).

Today we are seeing these Scriptures fulfilled before our eyes. Israel is a nation again and the Jews are returning to Israel in record numbers. A sign of the hastening of the prophetic time clock is when the Jews from the "north" of Israel (former Soviet Union) return to the land. Jeremiah 16:14-16 says once this happens, Jews from the entire world will return to Israel.

We are also beginning to see the spiritual fulfillment of this prophecy. The two covenant peoples of God, Jews and Christians, who have fought with each other, will unite under one King—Jesus. This will cause a spiritual explosion in the church.

The devil's worst nightmare will come to pass when

the sleeping giant, the church, finally realizes that the underlying purpose for the current outpourings of the Holy Spirit is to equip believers with power to evangelize the Jew. When the Jewish people join with the Gentiles to form One New Man, it will trigger a major release of power to evangelize the world! But before the church can enter this glorious future, it must first overcome its anti-Semitic past.

2

Christian?

The Fifth Commandment says, "Honor your father and your mother, that your days may be long upon the land…" (Exodus 20:12a). Scripture calls Abraham, Isaac, and Jacob the "fathers" of our faith (Romans 9:5). The church owes a debt of gratitude to the Jewish people. But if the church denies its Jewish heritage it is dishonoring its spiritual "fathers" and violating the commandment of God.

Malachi 4:6, the last prophecy in the Old Covenant, describes how important this matter is to God: "And he will turn the hearts of the fathers to the children, and the hearts of the children to their fathers, lest I come and strike the earth with a curse." If the "fathers" are the Jewish people, who are the "children?" The "children" represent Christians because they have received a spiritual heritage from the Jewish fathers of the faith. God says if the hearts of the Jewish people are not turned to the Christians and the hearts of the Christians to the Jewish people, He will strike the earth with a curse.

The devil has worked hard to keep the two groups apart. With cunning like a master chess player, he has placed a barrier that seems insurmountable between believers in Jesus and the Jewish people. Jesus came to break down the wall between Jew and Gentile. Ephesians 2:14 says, "For He Himself is our peace, who has made [Jew and Gentile] one, and **has broken down the middle wall of division.**"

Jesus prayed in John 17:21, "that they all may be one...that the world may believe." Whom does "all" refer to? It can't be Baptists and Presbyterians (or any other denomination). Why? They didn't exist at that time. He is praying for His followers, who were Jewish, and for those who will believe from their words, the Gentiles (v. 20). The stakes are high. Jesus says when Jewish and Gentile believers are one, the *world will believe!* When this happens, the same degree of glory that is on Jesus will be released on the church as Jesus stated in John 17:22: "And the glory which You gave Me I have given them, that they may be one just as We are one."

Not only will God's glory be released, but we will receive that same love that Father God has for Jesus. The Messiah said:

"And I have declared to them Your name, and will declare it, that the love with which You loved Me may be in them, and I in them" (John 17:26).

"Christian" Anti-Semitism

God has a marvelous plan for bringing about the unity of Jew and Gentile in Messiah Jesus. The apostle Paul writes, "To provoke [the Jews] to jealousy, salvation has come to the Gentiles" (Romans 11:11). God wants to use Gentiles to bring the Jewish people back into the Body of Messiah.

Somehow that truth has gotten lost. Provoking the Jew to jealousy means demonstrating supernatural peace, healing, strong family relationships, and love that only comes from intimacy with God. It means causing the Jew to want what believers have.

Instead of driving the Jewish people to jealousy, the church has simply driven them away. Although there are believers who have given their lives for the Jews,[1] some of the most anti-Jewish people in the last 2,000 years have been those who have called themselves Christians. Through the centuries, accusations and statements by church leaders against the Jews have led to a vicious form of "Christian" anti-Semitism. Here are a few examples:[2]

Justin Martyr (d. AD 167) was one of the first to accuse the Jews of inciting to kill Christians.

Origen (d. AD 254) accused Jews of plotting in their meetings to murder Christians.

Eusebius (c. AD 300) alleged that Jews, each year at the holiday of Purim, engaged in ceremonial killing of Christian children.

St. Hilary of Poitiers (d. AD 367) said that the Jews were a perverse people, forever accursed by God.

St. Ephraem (d. AD 373) wrote many of the early church hymns, some of which maligned Jews, even to the point of calling the Jewish synagogues "whorehouses."

St. John Chrysostom (AD 344-407) said that there could never be expiation for the Jews and that God had always hated them. He said it was "incumbent" upon all Christians to hate the Jews; they were assassins of Christ, and worshipers of the devil.

In one of his homilies, Chrysostom stated: "The synagogue is worse than a brothel...it is a den of scoundrels and the repair of wild beasts...the temple of demons devoted to idolatrous cults...the refuge of brigands and debauchees, and the cavern of devils."[3]

St. Cyril (d. AD 444) gave the Jews within his jurisdiction the choice of conversion, exile, or stoning.

St. Jerome (d. AD 420), translator of the Latin Vulgate, "proved" that Jews are incapable of understanding the Scriptures and said they should be severely persecuted until they confess the "true faith."

St. Augustine (d. AD 430) said the true image of the Jew was Judas Iscariot, forever guilty and ignorant spiritually. St. Augustine decided that Jews, for their own good and the good of society, must be relegated to the position of slaves. This theme was later picked up by *St. Thomas Aquinas* (d. AD 1274), who demanded that Jews be called to perpetual servitude.

According to Professor F. E. Talmage, St. Augustine believed that "because of their sin against Christ, the Jews rightly deserved death. Yet, as with Cain who murdered the just Abel, they are not to die.... For they are doomed to wander the earth...the 'witnesses of their iniquity and of our truth,' the living proof of Christianity."[4]

The Crusaders (AD 1099) herded Jews into the Great Synagogue in Jerusalem. When they were securely inside the locked doors, the synagogue was set on fire. And the misguided Crusaders, with the lies of perverted sermons fresh in their ears, sang as they marched around the blaze, "Christ, we adore Thee."

Martin Luther (c. 1544) said the Jews should not merely be slaves, but slaves of slaves, that they might not even come into contact with Christians. In his

The Last Lap

Schem Hamphoras, he said the Jews were ritual murderers and poisoners of wells. He called for all Talmuds and synagogues to be destroyed.

In his *Von den Juden und Iren Luegen* (1543), Luther wrote: "What then shall we Christians do with this damned, rejected race of Jews? Since they live among us and we know about their lying and blasphemy and cursing, we cannot tolerate them if we do not wish to share in their lies, curses, and blasphemy....We must prayerfully and reverentially practice a merciful severity."[5]

Encyclopaedia Judaica comments on Luther's statements: "Short of the Auschwitz oven and extermination, the whole Nazi Holocaust is pre-outlined here."[6] Indeed, Adolph Hitler wrote in *Mein Kampf*, "Hence today I believe that I am acting in accordance with the Almighty Creator: by defending myself against the Jew, I am fighting for the work of the Lord."[7]

Speaking as part of the church, we need a miracle. Only God can restore the damage between the church and the Jewish people. Repentance is the first step. We may not have been knowingly anti-Semitic, but as members of His Body, we must repent for the sins of the whole church. Daniel did not rebel against God, but he repented on behalf of Israel. Some feel we should not talk of this sad history. Then how can we ever repent and get clean?[8] The church must be rid of this horrible sin. Without holiness we will not see God (Hebrews 12:14).

All Israel Will Be Saved

Repentance will prepare the way for a great Jewish revival. God says, "For I do not desire, brethren, that you should be ignorant of this mystery...hardening in part has happened to Israel until the fullness [maturity] of the Gentiles has come in. And so all Israel will be saved" (Romans 11:25-26a). In other words, as the Gentiles who believe in Jesus get mature, the Jewish people will become open to the Gospel. Step one toward maturity involves repentance.

Thank God for the Passover Lamb who takes away the sins of the whole world!

---

[1] One example of a church leader who stood up for the Jewish people was Dietrich Bonhoeffer, a German Lutheran minister whose refusal to recant his opposition to Adolph Hitler's Nazi regime led to his imprisonment and eventual execution. He openly opposed not only the Nazi's anti-Jewish policies, but also the church's acquiescence to those policies.

[2] Unless otherwise noted, the following historical references are from Steffi Rubin, *Anti-Semitism* (Copyright Hineni Ministries, 1977), pp. 32-33.

[3] As cited in X. Malcolm Hay, *Europe and the Jews* (Boston: Beacon Press, 1961), p. 27.

[4] F. E. Talmage, ed., *Disputation and Dialogue: Readings in the Jewish-Christian Encounter* (New York: Ktav Publishing House, Inc., 1975), p. 18.

[5] As cited in *Encyclopaedia Judaica* (Jerusalem: Keter Publishing House Jerusalem Ltd., 1972), Vol. 8, p. 692.
Luther instructed "rulers who have Jewish subjects [to] exercise a sharp mercy toward these wretched people.... They must act like a good physician who, when gangrene has set in, proceeds without mercy to cut, saw, and burn flesh, veins, bone, and marrow.... Burn down their synagogues.... If this does not help we must drive them out like mad dogs...." From *Luther's Works, Vol. 47: The Christian in Society IV* (Philadelphia:

The Last Lap

Fortress Press, 1971), pp. 268-293. Excerpts cited in the *Internet Medieval Sourcebook* at www.fordham.edu/halshall/source/luther-jews.html.

[6] *Encyclopaedia Judaica* Vol. 8, p. 693.

[7] Adolph Hitler, *Mein Kampf*, translated by Ralph Manheim (Boston: Houghton Mifflin Co., 1971), p. 65.

[8] True repentance is not just saying you are sorry. It involves a change of behavior. Suggestions for true repentance will be explained in Chapter 4.

3

The Constantine Conspiracy

So a **curse** without **cause** shall not alight (Proverbs 26:2b).

C an a believer be under a curse for the anti-Semitic attitudes of his ancestors? Just ask Eric Carlson. While serving on a U.S. Navy submarine, Eric had a life-changing visitation from God that lasted for three days. The Lord revealed to him that he was Jewish. Eric later discovered that his grandfather had changed his last name when he immigrated to America in order to hide his Jewish identity.

Then God told Eric he was under a family curse for denying his Jewish heritage and that the curse had to be broken. After he prayed to break the curse, Eric was flooded with revelation and blessings.

God says He will bless those who bless the Jewish people and curse those who curse them (Genesis 12:3).

Mixture in God's House

Could the church be under a family curse like Eric was? Has the church denied its Jewish heritage? Yes. As we saw in the previous chapter, anti-Semitism has been a prominent part of church history for centuries. This didn't happen by accident. It was part of a deliberate plan to separate the church from anything Jewish. Let's call it for what it was—a conspiracy.

The first church was Jewish. If a Gentile wanted to follow the Messiah, he had to convert to Judaism. Then Peter had a revelation that Gentiles did not have to become Jews to be saved (Acts 10). The Jerusalem Council meeting determined that Gentiles did not have to be circumcised. There were only four easily followed requirements. They were to "abstain from things polluted by idols, from sexual immorality, from things strangled, and from blood" (Acts 15:20). This opened the door to widespread church growth among the Gentiles. So many were saved that the Jewish believers became a minority.

The first Jewish followers of Jesus were called Nazarenes. They practiced traditional Judaism and were widely accepted by non-believing Jews. Early in the second century their numbers reached 400,000.[1] In the book of Acts, the early church fathers said to Paul: "You see, brother, how many myriads [tens of thousands] of Jews there are who have believed, and they are all zealous for the law" (21:20b).

The Nazarenes' acceptance by traditional Jews came to a halt in AD 135 when Rabbi Akiba declared that Bar Kochba was the Jewish Messiah. His followers hoped he would lead them to victory over the Romans. The Nazarenes refused to fight because they believed Jesus was the true Messiah rather than Bar Kochba. They were branded traitors, *not* because they believed in Jesus, but because they wouldn't join Bar Kochba's armed struggle. Bar Kochba and his followers were quickly slaughtered by the Romans. Afterward, Jews were banned from Jerusalem.

History shows that as the center of the Christian faith moved from Jerusalem to Rome, it became increasingly Hellenized, adopting pagan customs and philosophies rather than the God-ordained practices and beliefs of the Bible. At the same time Christianity became increasingly anti-Jewish.

In AD 196, when no Jewish believers were present, a church council meeting in Caesarea changed the celebration of Jesus' resurrection from the third day of Passover (Firstfruits, Leviticus 23:9-11; 1 Corinthians 15:4,20-23) to Sunday, during the feast of the pagan fertility goddess, Ishtar. In the fourth century, the Council of Nicea made the change official. The decision was based on the premise that it was not proper for the church in her celebrations to be connected with "the cursed Jewish nation" that crucified Him.[2]

Today, the holiday is known as Easter (from Ishtar). Have you ever wondered why we have Easter bunnies and eggs? These are vestiges of Ishtar (the fertility goddess) worship.

Whatever Happened to the Sabbath?

Another reform by the Council of Nicea (headed by the Roman Emperor Constantine) "institutionalized" the switch of the day of Christian worship from Saturday to Sunday. As with Easter, the change had actually started much earlier. In fact, by the middle of the second century, Sunday, the day devoted to the sun god, had largely replaced Saturday, the day devoted to the One true God.

The Sabbath was the first element of creation that God had sanctified, or set apart, in remembrance of His creative power. That God had rested on the Sabbath day was a biblical fact. Nevertheless, the change was made and justified by the church leaders, and not initially on the basis of the resurrection. The primary rationale for the observance of Sunday was to commemorate the first day of creation. The resurrection of Jesus was only a secondary issue.

Many of the church leaders who originally changed the Sabbath day were anti-Semitic. Tertullian thought that God had always hated the Sabbath.[3] The Epistle of Barnabas (apocryphal literature from the first century AD) denies altogether that God had ever given the Sabbath as a commandment to be kept. Justin Martyr (d. AD 167) considered the Sabbath to be a highly deserved curse on the Jewish people.

Martyr lectured Trypho the Jew by saying, "It was by reason of your sins and the sins of your Fathers that, among other precepts, God imposed upon you the observance of the Sabbath as a mark." This "mark" was to "single them out for the punishment they so well deserved for their infidelities."[4]

Instead of recognizing that "the Sabbath was made for man" (Mark 2:27), the Sabbath was seen as part of the curse of the law, upon that hated and despised race—the Jews. The post-apostolic church instituted another day of worship to separate themselves from all things Jewish. This anti-Judaism was reflected in the Replacement Theology (belief that the church has replaced Israel) of the early writers of the Hellenized church. (See Appendix A, "Is the Church the 'New Israel'?" for a more complete discussion of Replacement Theology).

Constantine, a Roman Emperor who came to power

early in the fourth century (AD 306-337), was a master politician. He tried to satisfy heathens and Christians by modifying pagan customs and festivals and giving them Christian meanings. The group he didn't like was the Jews since they had rebelled against Rome. And the church was more than willing to follow Constantine's lead in order to avoid persecution. Christians were prohibited from worshiping on Saturday or observing Passover, upon the threat of excommunication or worse.

Constantine expressed the anti-Judaic sentiments of the bishops of the Christian world when he wrote: "Let us therefore have nothing in common with this odious people, the Jews, for we have received from our Savior a different way…. Strive and pray continually that the purity of your souls may not be sullied by fellowship with the customs of these most wicked men…. All should unite in desiring that which sound reason appears to demand in avoiding all participation in the perjured conduct of the Jews."[5]

Too Cold

Another major change started early in church history was the celebration of Christmas. Today it is the most hallowed religious holiday next to Easter. But was Jesus born on December 25th? We know He was not according to Luke 2:8. Shepherds would not have been out in the field watching their flocks *at night* in Bethlehem in December (winter season) because it would have been too cold.

It makes more sense that Jesus was born about the time of Sukkot (Feast of Tabernacles). This feast is referred to as "the Season of Our Joy." What greater joy than for Messiah to tabernacle with man?

Scripture tells us that the law, which includes biblical festivals, is a "shadow of the good things to come" (Hebrews 10:1). Sukkot foreshadows the dwelling of God with man. "And the Word became flesh and dwelt [tabernacled] among us" (John 1:14). The Feast of Tabernacles provides a much better picture of Jesus than Christmas.

So where did December 25th come from? Babylonian pagans believed the sun was god. The winter solstice began on December 21st and represented the death of the sun. By December 25th, the sun's climb in the sky and a wild celebration of its "rebirth" took place. This rebirth celebration was in honor of the incarnation of the sun god and his mother, the "queen of heaven." To draw pagans into Christianity, the Roman Catholic Church proclaimed December 25th to be the birthday of the Messiah, although this is not mentioned in Scripture. The festival was called "Christ's Masse" and was later shortened to "Christmas."[6] The early Puritans knew this history and did not celebrate Christmas.[7]

The Last Lap

Where's the Power?

It's no coincidence that when the Jewish biblical heritage of the church was replaced with paganism, intimacy with God was watered down. The church went from everyone doing the works of Jesus to professional clergy leading a congregation of spectators. The supernatural power of God was replaced with the politics and traditions of men.[8]

When the church walked away from its biblical Jewish roots, it abandoned God's pattern. The original "church split" was the division between Jew and Gentile. It was a literal divorce. And God hates divorce (Malachi 2:16). When we remove the wall dividing Jew and Gentile, we will break the curse off of the church and clear the way for widespread revival.

---

[1]Raymond Robert Fischer, *The Children of God: Messianic Jews and Gentile Christians Nourished by Common Jewish Roots* (Tiberias, Israel: Olim Publications, 2000), p. 47.

[2]Lars Enarson, "The Feast of Passover and Intercession for Salvation of the Jewish People: An Appeal for an All Night Prayer Vigil on April 7 or 8, 2001" (The Watchman International, P.O. Box 3670, Pensacola, FL 32516, 1999), pp. 1-2.

[3]Against Marcion 1, p. 271 ANF III.

[4]Dialogue 21,1; 23,3.

[5]Theodoret, Historia Ecclesiastica 1,10.

[6]"In the fifth century the western church [Roman Catholic] ordered it to be celebrated forever on the day of the old Roman feast of the birth of Sol [sun]" *The Encyclopedia Americana*, 1942 Edition, Vol. 6, p. 623.

[7]*Century Dictionary and Cyclopedia*, 1903, Vol. 2, p. 987.

[8]See Fischer's book for a more detailed history of the first church.

4

Biblical Festivals:
Bondage or Blessing?

God says that at the time of the fullness of the
Gentiles, the Jewish people will be grafted back into
their *own* olive tree (Romans 11:24-25). Isn't it time
the Body of Messiah started to look like the Jewish
olive tree?

Before Jesus came to earth, the only covenant
which provided for atonement for sin was between
God and the Jewish people. If a Gentile wanted to follow God, he had to become a proselyte to Judaism.
The prophet Jeremiah predicted a new and better
covenant that would wash away sins and allow us to
know God (31:31-34). But this covenant, fulfilled in

Messiah Jesus, is also "only" with the Jewish people. So, in effect, the only way to have your sins forgiven and to know God is to participate in a Jewish covenant based on the blood of the Jewish Messiah as prophesied in the Jewish Scriptures by the Jewish prophets.

Yet, when a Jew looks at Christianity today, he sees little or nothing that appears to be Jewish. When a Christian looks at Judaism, he sees a belief system that differs radically from Christianity. Jesus came to break down the middle wall of partition and create from Jew and Gentile One New Man:

> For He Himself is our peace, who has made both one, and has broken down the middle wall of division between us, having abolished in His flesh the enmity, that is, the law of commandments contained in ordinances, so as to create in Himself one new man from the two, thus making peace (Ephesians 2:14-15).

Today, nearly 2,000 years after Paul wrote these words, there is an even greater wall of separation.

The big lie the devil tells Jewish people is that they can't be Jewish and believe in Jesus. By hiding its Jewish roots the church has reinforced this lie. It is time for Jewish people and Christians alike to see

Biblical Festivals: Bondage or Blessing?

Christianity's Jewish connection. As a means of reinforcing this, I will refer to Jesus by His Hebrew name, "Yeshua," for the remainder of the book.

Under the Law?

The first church observed all the biblical festivals. During the Millennium (the thousand-year reign of Yeshua on earth) we will observe the Sabbath (Isaiah 66:23) and the Feast of Tabernacles (Zechariah 14:16-17). Why have we put these celebrations "on hold" for centuries?

One reason is that many resist anything that appears to put them "under the law." Paul makes it clear that we are not justified by the law (Romans 3:20, Ephesians 2:8-9). But does this mean the law has no value? Should we disregard such laws as the Ten Commandments? Of course not. Paul proclaimed, "Therefore the law is holy, and the commandment holy and just and good" (Romans 7:12).

Yeshua explained this paradox in Matthew 5:18: "Till heaven and earth pass away, one jot or one tittle will by no means pass from the law till all is fulfilled." The key word is *fulfilled.* This word is best understood by reversing the syllables of "fulfilled" to "filled full." Yeshua is the full meaning of the law. He did not come to eliminate the law but to enable us to fill it full of its true meaning.

The Last Lap

Yeshua was never upset with the Torah (first five books of the Bible). He said, "Do not think that I came to destroy the Law [Torah] or the Prophets. I did not come to destroy but to fulfill" (Matthew 5:17). What He *did* object to were the ways in which the rabbis would cleverly overrule many portions of the Torah. Yeshua asked, "Why do you also transgress the commandment of God because of your tradition?" (Matthew 15:3).

Before you conclude that I am advocating a new form of legalism, let's get one thing straight. Celebrating the Jewish biblical feasts has nothing to do with obtaining salvation or righteousness. This was the mistake of the Judaizers in the book of Galatians. Repentance and the blood of Yeshua save us. Nothing more is needed. However, observing the festivals is a matter of *blessing*.

Appointment with the President
So what should be our attitude toward the biblical feasts? The Hebrew word for "feasts" is *mo'ed*, which means "appointed times." Leviticus 23:2 makes it clear that these are not only Jewish feasts, they are *God's* feasts. In other words, these are God's appointed times to meet with us. Would you ignore or arrive late for your set time to meet with the President of the United States? It wouldn't cost you your salvation, but

you would miss a great honor and blessing. How much more of a blessing would you miss if you stood God up at His set appointment? God calls the feasts, "convocations," which in the Hebrew means "rehearsals" (Leviticus 23:2). God says we should observe these rehearsals at His appointed times *forever* (Leviticus 23:14,21,31,41). Since the festivals were such clear shadows of Yeshua's first coming, they must hold significant keys to His return. We should observe the feasts (fulfill them) as great celebrations. It is as if God is throwing a party and inviting us to attend. There is so much revelation about Yeshua ready to be released as we worship God at these appointed times.

Passover

Looking at the Passover dinner gives us insight about the last days. The first New Covenant Passover was actually an "engagement dinner." It was not just to remember the Exodus from Egypt, but it was a promise of a future exodus from earth. In ancient Judaism an engagement was as binding as a marriage. After the engagement, the bridegroom went to prepare a room in His father's house for his bride.

At the Last Supper, Yeshua drank the third cup of wine—"the cup of redemption," which He called the "new covenant in My blood" (Luke 22:20).[1] In the context of the marriage customs of ancient Israel, He was also making a kind of betrothal statement. Earlier, He had told His disciples:

> "I go to prepare a place for you. And if I go and prepare a place for you, I will come again, and receive you to Myself; that where I am, there you may be also" (John 14:2b,3).

The custom in those days was for a bridegroom to pay a price, either in goods or services, to the father of his bride as compensation for the loss of her presence in their household. In drinking the cup of redemption Yeshua was saying to His bride, the church, "I will redeem you—I will pay the price for you." Yeshua's blood on the cross was the highest price ever paid for a bride. It released the Holy Spirit to assemble this new bride made up of Jews and Gentiles who become One New Man in Yeshua.

The fourth cup of wine we drink at the Passover meal is called "the cup of praise." Yeshua did not drink this cup on earth. After the third cup, He said,

> "But I say unto you, I will not drink of this fruit of the vine from now on until that day when I drink it new with you in My Father's kingdom" (Matthew 26:29).

Biblical Festivals: Bondage or Blessing?

That day will come when the church, the One New Man Bride, is caught up in the air to be with Yeshua (1 Thessalonians 4:16-17). We will share with Him in the Marriage Supper of the Lamb—a heavenly Passover meal (Revelation 19:7-9).

Blessing, Not Bondage

As a traditional Jew I used to follow the festivals the same way each year. Eventually, I got bored with traditions learned by rote. When I became a Messianic Jew I found there were hidden meanings about the Messiah in the festivals. I saw purpose in the celebrations. But observing the same events exactly the same way year after year again became boring. It became more of a form of entertainment or tradition than a spiritual encounter with God.

So what is the answer? We should not necessarily follow the rabbinic interpretations and traditions or even our new Messianic understandings exactly the same way every time. Instead, we should study each festival in the Scriptures. Then pray, "Holy Spirit, how can we glorify Yeshua in a special way at this appointed time?"[2]

Yeshua performed more miracles on the Sabbath than on any other day. I have found that God increases the anointing for miracles and evangelism during the festivals. When you celebrate these feasts, you feel God's pleasure.

I believe there are supernatural blessings connected with observing the biblical festivals in liberty. For instance, God specifically states that for those who observe the Sabbath, "I will give you great honor and give you your full share of the inheritance I promised to Jacob, your ancestor. I, the LORD, have spoken!" (Isaiah 58:14, NLT).

Churches are beginning to use the seven biblical festivals as corporate worship events: Passover, Unleavened Bread, First Fruits, Pentecost, Trumpets, Day of Atonement, and Tabernacles. I see the day coming when the largest football stadiums will not be able to hold all the believers at these celebrations.

We are told to teach the festivals to our children (Exodus 12:26-27). I believe God would be honored if we set the Sabbath apart for family time. Because of His supernatural promises, God will use this time to restore families. What a great way for Yeshua to fulfill ("fill full" of Himself) the Fourth Commandment.

Unholy Merger

Prophets such as Jeremiah and Hosea forbade the Jewish people to merge paganism with belief in God (Jeremiah 7:30-31, Hosea 3:1). Jeremiah 2:13 says the people have committed two evils. They have forsaken God's vessel and made their own vessels that leak.

Biblical Festivals: Bondage or Blessing?

In the early church, Jewish believers in the Messiah were forced by Gentile Christians to give up worship on the Sabbath and other biblical festivals under threat of excommunication or death. As we saw in the previous chapter, these godly shadows and prophetic pictures of the Messiah's first coming, return, and Millennial Kingdom were replaced with pagan traditions.

What are we to do today? Are we to give up Sunday worship? Not necessarily. The key is not that we should abandon Sunday as a day of worship, but that we should repent of the anti-Semitic attitudes of the early church leaders who established Sunday worship.

Doesn't the Bible tell us to worship on Sunday? No. The Bible mentions some gathered on the first day of the week. One reason for this was because tithes and alms giving and all business could not be conducted on the Sabbath. Nowhere in Scripture are we *commanded* to worship on Sunday.

Many refer to Sunday, as "the Lord's Day," giving it special significance as a holy day. What is the Lord's Day? Psalm 118:24 says, **"This** is the day which the LORD has made; we will rejoice and be glad in it." Today most Christians worship the Lord on Sunday. But God has selected *every* day to be the day the Lord has made or the "Lord's Day." Since Sunday is usually a day we do not have to work, it is a convenient time for corporate worship. However, that doesn't make it the Sabbath.

Celebrating in Joy and Freedom
Hosea 3:4-5 says:

> For the children of Israel shall abide many days without king or prince, without sacrifice or sacred pillar, without ephod or teraphim. Afterward the children of Israel shall return, seek the LORD their God and David their king.

In other words, in the latter days there will be a revival among the Jewish people. This is the set time to favor Zion (Israel) (Psalm 102:13).

True repentance, or change in behavior, by the church will release this Jewish revival. What would demonstrate true repentance on behalf of the Gentile Christians for the anti-Semitism of the church and forcing the Jewish believers to reject their biblical festivals? Reconciliation meetings have been a good start, but we need to go deeper. Not much has changed. Israel is not saved. What about a step of repentance by restoring the Jewish roots of the faith?

Some congregations will worship only on the Sabbath, which is also known as the Shabbat. The bib-

lical Shabbat begins on Friday evening at sundown
Other congregations will worship on Shabbat and
Sunday. Instead of a Sunday morning service and a
Sunday evening service, how about a Friday evening
and a Sunday morning service? I'm not suggesting a
rigid tradition. Pray and do what is pleasing to God.
Do not make the Shabbat a legalistic formula. "The
Sabbath was made for man, and not man for the
Sabbath" (Mark 2:27). At the same time, do not act as
if Sunday worship is a legalistic formula. Never lose
sight of the objective. The objective is not Jewish
roots, but the Jewish Messiah, who is our Sabbath.

Warning: If you think this is just another segmented
ministry of the church such as a singles group or just
another meeting like Wednesday night prayer, you
have missed the Spirit of God. The idea behind a
Shabbat service is for the congregation to totally identify with its biblical roots and with the Jewish people
and the Jewish Messiah. If the majority attend on
Sunday and just a few on Shabbat, you will end up
with two congregations. God is after One New Man,
not a few segregated events.

Some will take the revelation of Jewish roots and
pagan mixture in Christianity and create a legalistic
system based on a works mentality. Eventually, these
Judaizers will evolve into a denomination and fos-
silize. A religious spirit will settle on them. Their iden-

tity will be in their Jewish culture rather than the Jewish Messiah. They will cause much disunity in the Body. Many in the church will fight this "religious" Jewish roots movement because of the legalists. The devil tries to get us in a religious ditch on one side of the road or the other. But a new move of God's Spirit will blow on the church and a new freedom in biblical festivals will come forth. And no weapon formed against it will prosper. It will be marked by joy and freedom.

———————

[1]A traditional understanding of the Passover seder ties the four cups of wine to the four "I will" statements of Exodus 6:6-7: "Therefore say to the children of Israel: 'I am the LORD; I will bring you out from under the burdens of the Egyptians, I will rescue you from their bondage, and I will redeem you with an outstretched arm and with great judgments. I will take you as My people, and I will be your God....'" "I will redeem you" is the third statement, which corresponds to the third cup.

[2]You can order two excellent books on the biblical feasts from Messianic Vision: *The Family Guide to the Jewish Holidays*, available for $35, and *The Feasts of the Lord*, available for $25.

5

The Rabbinic Conspiracy

A friend of mine, the pastor of a large Charismatic church, had a supernatural experience while he was visiting the Great Synagogue in Jerusalem. As he was praying, Yeshua came to him and said, "I would be more at home in this building than in your church."

Many Gentile believers, longing for their biblical Jewish heritage, feel a similar discomfort with church. But is the solution to be found in adding rabbinic Judaism to our belief in Yeshua?

No. Simply put, rabbinic Judaism has drifted far afield from the Judaism of the Bible. Tradition in the church may have insulated Christians from the full intimacy and power of God and from their biblical roots. But the tradition of the rabbis has separated

Jewish people from their Messiah.

While the devil was making the church leaders anti-Semitic, he was corrupting the authority of the Scriptures in Judaism. Both groups were digging in and believing the big lie—you can't be Jewish and believe in Yeshua. The formula was simple. Give the rabbis authority above the Scriptures. Remove Yeshua from Judaism and separate the Christian from the Jew. This will stop the unlimited outpouring of God's glory. And the full revival will be aborted.

A New Religion

Let's examine how rabbinic Judaism has tried to exclude Yeshua. In the Great Revolt by Jewish Zealots against Roman rule (AD 66-70), a million Jews were killed and the temple in Jerusalem was destroyed. Afterward, Yohanan ben Zakkai set about to reconstruct Judaism in Yavne on the coast of Israel. Why was this necessary? Because there was no temple and they had rejected God's Messiah—the sacrifice that was made once for all. The Torah (first five books of the Old Covenant) clearly says that without the shedding of blood, there is no remission of sin (Leviticus 17:11). Rather than accept the truth that animal sacrifices were a shadow of the ultimate Passover Lamb—the Messiah—who would take away all sin, ben Zakkai and his followers invented a new bloodless religion—rabbinic Judaism.

The following quote illustrates the dramatic shift that took place within Judaism:

> As Rabban Yohanan ben Zakkai was coming forth from Jerusalem, Rabbi Joshua followed after him and beheld the Temple in ruins. "Woe unto us!" Rabbi Joshua cried, "that this, the place where the iniquities of Israel were atoned for is laid waste!" "My son," Rabban Yohanan said to him, "be not grieved; we have another atonement as effective as this. And what is it? It is acts of loving-kindness, as it is said, 'For I desire mercy and not sacrifice' [Hosea 6:6]" (Avot de Rabbi Nathan 4:18).[1]

At the end of his life, ben Zakkai finally realized his creation gave him no assurance of life in the age to come. On his death bed, he said: "I have before me two roads, one to Paradise and one to Gehenna [hell], and I know not whether [God] will sentence me to Gehenna or admit me to Paradise" (Tractate Berachot 28b). A famous rabbi said, "If the blind leads the blind, both will fall into a ditch" (Matthew 15:14b).

Rabbi Akiba ben Joseph studied the teachings of Yohanan ben Zakkai in Yavne and continued to build on his foundation. He created the structure of the Talmud, which is a declaration of rabbinic authority.

Although the Talmud contains a good deal of wisdom and godly teaching, one of the major goals of its authors was to keep the Jew from believing in Messiah Yeshua. It distorts many of the Messianic interpretations of the Jewish Scriptures. There is clear evidence that *before* Yeshua came to earth the Jewish people were expecting a Messiah and interpreted the Messianic prophecies without bias.

Today, the rabbis claim the Talmud, or Oral Law, came from God at the same time the Written Law was given to Moses on Mount Sinai. This is not true. Even in the first century, Jewish leaders did not claim rabbinic law came from Sinai. Instead they spoke of "oral traditions." The Jewish Bible, the Dead Sea Scrolls, and the Jewish historian Josephus (AD 93) do not even mention an oral law.

The method of interpreting Scripture employed by Akiba and his followers rejected the rules of grammar and plain logic. Author Dan Gruber writes, "Sometimes the Rabbis were unable to read their teachings into the Scriptures by any means. So they simply annulled the decrees of Torah."[2]

They proclaimed rabbinic authority took precedence over the Scriptures.[3] The Talmud states, "My son, take heed of the words of the Scribes more than the words of the Torah."[4] Akiba's objective was to bring the Jewish people under the rule of the rabbis.

The Talmud even says that if a voice from heaven contradicts the majority of the rabbis, the rabbis are correct.[5] No one is allowed to contradict the authority of the rabbis, not even God!

Is it any wonder that, between persecution from the church and the rabbinic conspiracy, Jewish people know nothing about Yeshua?

Who is the Messiah?

In modern times the rabbis have missed two of the most significant events to happen to the Jewish people in the last 2,000 years. Messianic Jewish author Ron Cantor notes that many rabbis initially opposed the creation of Israel as a modern Jewish nation. "Many of the rabbis of Jerusalem were actually siding with the Arabs to keep this from happening. They believed only the Messiah could set up a Jewish state."[6] They also vehemently opposed Eliezer Ben Yehuda's plans to restore Hebrew as the national language of the Jewish people in the late 1800s.

Cantor notes, "If it was so clear to the rabbis that both the Jewish state and the Hebrew language were the dreams of false prophets and yet they were wrong, it is possible that they also missed it on the single most important issue in Judaism—The Messiah!"[7]

The Last Lap

Does Isaiah 53 Speak of Yeshua?

The rabbis have tried to prevent the Jewish people from believing in Yeshua by removing Isaiah 53 from the regular synagogue readings. It is in the accepted Jewish Scriptures (Tenach). Isaiah recorded this prophecy seven centuries before Yeshua was born. Why is it not read in the synagogues? Because any Jew who thinks for himself would recognize it speaks of Yeshua.

When I share this passage with rabbis, some say they are not holy enough and must read what the rabbis had to say about it in the past. But they don't go back far enough. They only consult the rabbis after Yeshua—the ones who distorted Scripture. The rabbis before Yeshua were not prejudiced and saw the Messianic significance of this passage.[8] Others insult my intelligence by saying the prophet is speaking of Israel rather than Yeshua. Yet, Isaiah 53:8-9 says the One who would die for the sins of the world would have no sin of His own. This could not be Israel. There are numerous places in Scripture where the prophets point out Israel's sins. No nation is sinless before God.

When my own Orthodox Jewish father read Isaiah 53, he knew immediately that the prophet was describing Yeshua—despite being taught all his life that Yeshua was *not* the Jewish Messiah.

Think for Yourself

Jeremiah predicted a new covenant that would wipe away sins and allow us to know (have intimacy with) God (31:31-34). The Jewish Scriptures tell us that the Messiah would be born in Bethlehem (Micah 5:2). He would be raised from the dead (Psalm 16:10). Daniel 9:26 makes it clear that He would die before the second temple was destroyed. Since it was destroyed in AD 70, He had to come, die, and be resurrected before that time! And Isaiah 11:10 tells us the Gentiles will follow the Jewish Messiah.

What other person do you know of who was born in Bethlehem, who was followed by the Gentiles, who was sacrificed for our sins before the destruction of the second temple, and who was raised from the dead?

The powerful prophecies listed above are from the approved Jewish Scriptures and are written out in Appendix B. Please take a moment to read these verses and to have your own God encounter.

---

[1] As cited in Kevin Howard and Marvin Rosenthal, *The Feasts of the Lord* (Nashville: Thomas Nelson Publishers, 1997), p. 126.

[2] Dan Gruber, *Rabbi Akiba's Messiah* (Hanover, NH: Elijah Publishing, 1999), p. 80. Gruber's book provides an excellent history of the origins of Rabbinic Judaism.

[3] Ibid.

[4] Erubin 21b in J. M. Baumgarten, "The Unwritten Law in the Pre-Rabbinic Period," *Journal for the Study of Judaism in the Persian, Hellenistic and Roman Period*, Vol. III, Oct. 1972, p. 23 as cited in Gruber, p. 107.

The Last Lap

[5]Gruber, pp. 111, 116-118.

[6]Ron Cantor, *I Am Not Ashamed* (Gaithersburg, MD: Tikkun International, 1999), p. 140-141).

[7]Cantor, p. 142.

[8]For the commentaries of the rabbis before Yeshua and the revisionary views of the modern rabbis on the major Messianic prophecies, read Philip Moore, *The End of History, Messiah Conspiracy* (Atlanta: Ramshead Press International, 1996).

6

Who Is Israel?

My friend, Dr. Derek Prince, wrote, "Almost limitless misunderstanding, ignorance and distortion have pervaded the church for many centuries concerning the identity of Israel. This seems extraordinary to me because the statements in the Bible regarding Israel are so clear. Nevertheless, the minds of multitudes of Christians seem to be clouded in regard to the application of the name *Israel.*"[1] Dr. Prince has also said that a Christian who has no particular love for the Jew and Israel is "deficient" and "incomplete."[2]

Replacement Theology is a teaching that says the church has replaced Israel in God's eyes and inherited its blessings while the Jews are cursed. Under this logic Scripture is interpreted by replacing references to Israel with the words, "the church." A reading of Romans 9-11 will demonstrate to us the need to *replace* Replacement Theology. The promises to the Jewish people are *irrevocable!* (See Appendix A: "Is the Church the 'New Israel'?" for a more complete discussion of Replacement Theology.)

One example of the many passages that disprove this theology is found in Romans 11:28-29. If, as some claim, the church has replaced Israel, we should be able to read the passage as follows:

"Concerning the gospel they [the church] are enemies for your sake, but concerning the election they [the church] are beloved for the sake of the fathers. For the gifts and the calling of God are irrevocable."

Can an honest, literal reading justify interpreting "they" as "the church?" Is the church opposed to the Gospel or is Israel opposed? Is the church beloved for the promises to the fathers (Abraham, Isaac, and Jacob) or is Israel beloved?

Some Gentile believers say, "I feel Jewish. I have such a love for Jewish people and Jewish festivals, I must have Jewish blood." Your reaction is normal. After all, you have the blood of Yeshua, the greatest Jew who ever lived, flowing through your veins. If you *did not* have a supernatural love for the Jew and Israel, I would question whether you know Yeshua. However, this does not make you a physical Jew.

One Gentile Christian I know thinks that because she *might* have one ancestor over the past 2,000 years who was of the lost tribes of Israel, she is an Israelite or an "Ephraimite." She bases her belief on allegorical interpretations of Scripture rather than the literal. But we have no right to spiritualize God's Word if our interpretation contradicts the literal meaning.

Let's start with simple definitions. The word "Hebrew" was first used to identify Abram's (Abraham's) family (Genesis 14:13). It was Abraham's grandson, Jacob, who was first called "Israel" after he wrestled with God (Genesis 32:28). Later, the nation of Israel was divided into two sections, the southern tribes of Judah and Benjamin, and the ten northern tribes. A "Jew" is literally a physical descendant from the tribe of Judah. An "Israelite" is a descendant from the ten northern tribes. However, God calls both Judah and Ephraim, "Israel" in Ezekiel 37:16. Today the term "Jew" is used to identify all the physical seed of Abraham through his son, Isaac. Paul, who was from the tribe of Benjamin, called himself a Jew, an Israelite, and a Hebrew (Philippians 3:5, Acts 21:39, and Romans 11:1), proving all three terms are used interchangeably.

The Last Lap

Are You Jealous?

Why do so many Christians believe they have replaced Israel? Why do so many Gentile believers want to be Jewish or to call themselves Israel or Ephraim?[3] Why do they need to be the physical seed of Abraham when they are in *the spiritual seed* of Abraham through Yeshua? Why would they want to miss their destiny? Jews need Gentile believers. And Gentile believers need Jews.

Ruth understood this. If this Gentile had not attached herself to Naomi the Jew, she would have never met Boaz. The fruit of this marriage produced Obed, the grandfather of King David. Yeshua was descended from King David.

If Esther, the Jew, did not marry King Ahasuerus, the Gentile, the Jewish people would have perished. When the Jews were spared, it sparked a revival among the Gentiles. The book of Esther says many became Jews (Esther 8:17).

There will be no One New Man without the Gentile fulfilling his destiny. Salvation has come to the Gentile to evangelize the Jews (Romans 11:11b). When the Jews are saved it will literally bring life from the dead (Romans 11:15). The One New Man will cause the dead religious church to explode with the glory of God!

The blindness on the eyes of the Gentile church is

as supernatural as the blindness on the eyes of the Jewish people. The jealousy is demonic. The parable of the prodigal son illustrates this spiritual truth. You may have heard other applications of this parable, but this is what God has shown me.

The younger son is a type of the Jewish people. The older son is a type of the Gentile church. When the younger son returned home, the father (a type of Father God) held a great celebration with food, *music* and *dancing*. The older brother was jealous. Luke 15:28 says that he "was angry [with deep-seated wrath] and resolved not to go in" (Amp.). He didn't understand the One New Man. He didn't realize that the Jew must be grafted into the Body of Messiah in order to have the Wedding Supper of the Lamb (the heavenly feast enjoyed by the Messiah and His Bride, the church). The older brother couldn't comprehend the truth expressed by Yeshua that He would not return until the Jewish people were restored to the Father (Matthew 23:39). He couldn't see that by being in the seed of Abraham, *everything the father had was his* (Luke 15:31).

When the Jew comes back to the Father, God will bring a new type of music and dancing into the church. Religious Gentiles, who are stuck in their traditions, will be angry over this new wave of worship and will refuse to participate.

The Last Lap

After 2,000 years of living with the pigs (the younger brother ended up feeding the pigs), we Jewish believers have a lot of rough edges. Gentile Christians (older brother) have a sweetness because of generations of knowing the Messiah. We Jewish believers desperately need to be embraced by our older brothers.

There is one Body. The Body of Messiah is not Messianic Jewish and Gentile Christian. It is not having joint meetings. There is no wall of separation! When God sees the Body, He doesn't see Jew and Gentile but He sees His Son, Yeshua. He is the One New Man, the King of the Jews!

Warning Judgments

The question of God's calling on the Jew and Israel is just as important for our nation to understand as it is for the church. The United States, as a nation, has violated every one of the Ten Commandments. We are hanging by a single thread. One of the main reasons we still enjoy some of God's favor is because we have been a friend to Israel. However, we are dangerously close to losing that blessing. God always warns before judgment to allow for repentance. He is giving His final warning to America.

Zechariah 2:8-9 states:

"Anyone who harms you [Israel] harms my most

precious possession. I [God] will raise my fist to crush them…" (NLT).

John McTernan, in his book, *God's Final Warning to America,* documents that when America has gone against Israel we have suffered "warning judgments."[4] Former President George Bush initiated his 1991 peace plan for the Middle East right after the Gulf War. As part of that plan, he tried to pressure Israel to surrender land for peace. God promised this land to the Jewish people forever. Is it just a coincidence that, despite enjoying high approval ratings after the Gulf War, Bush went on to lose his bid for re-election?

When the United States pressures Israel to give away her land, warning judgments befall America almost simultaneously! Proverbs 26:2b says, "So a curse without cause shall not alight."

On October 30, 1991, former President Bush gave a speech to open the "land for peace" conference in Madrid, Spain. The next day, one of the most powerful storms to have ever occurred in the United States smashed into New England. The storm damaged the East Coast from Maine to Florida. Thirty-foot waves pounded President Bush's home in Kennebunkport, Maine, inflicting heavy damage. Later a book and movie came out about this massive storm called, "The Perfect Storm."

The Last Lap

On August 23, 1992, the Madrid Peace Conference was transferred to Washington D.C. The very first day of the conference Hurricane Andrew hit southern Florida. Andrew was the worst natural disaster ever to hit the United States!

In January 1998, President Bill Clinton met with Israeli Prime Minister Benjamin Netanyahu to pressure him to give up land for peace. Soon after, while Clinton was waiting for a meeting with Yasser Arafat, the nation learned of the sex scandal that led to his impeachment.

These are just a few of the many warnings. If these are just the warnings, imagine what the judgments will be like! God is serious. Time is running short.

---

[1]Derek Prince, *Prophetic Destinies* (Altamonte Springs, FL: Creation House, 1992), p. 13.

[2]See the Foreword to Sid Roth, *Time Is Running Short* (Shippensburg, PA: Destiny Image Publishers, 1990).

[3]Over the years some have objected to my use of the term, "Gentile Christian." I meet many Christians who are ashamed of their Gentile heritage and wish they were Jewish. Some feel that the term "Gentile" is even derogatory. While the word "Gentiles" has sometimes been associated with "heathen," it is better defined as "nations" or "non-Jews"—a distinct people group. The term is neutral. There are good Gentiles and bad Gentiles, just as there are good Jews and bad Jews. Besides, Paul would not have addressed non-Jewish believers as "Gentiles" if it were an insult (Romans 11:13, 16:4, and Galatians 2:12,14).

Should we let unbelievers define our identity? Although I am a new creation in Yeshua, I am not ashamed of my Jewish heritage. If I were a Gentile, I would not be ashamed of my Gentile heritage. But I would be proud of my identity. Our *heritage* is Jewish or Gentile, but our *identity* is Yeshua!

[4]John McTernan, *God's Final Warning to America* (Oklahoma City: Hearthstone Publishing, 2000), pp. 82-119. This book is available from Messianic Vision for $14, postage paid.

7

"We Are Not Lost"

It is a miracle that Jewish people still exist today. After thousands of years of not having a country or temple and being persecuted wherever they went, there should be none left. But God said as long as there is a sun and moon and stars, there will be a physical Jew on the face of the earth (Jeremiah 31:35-36).

We know that during His Millennial Reign, Yeshua and His disciples will rule over the twelve tribes of Israel (Matthew 19:28). The ancient rabbis believed three things had to take place before the Messiah would appear. First, Israel had to be restored as a Jewish nation. This occurred in 1948. Second, the temple had to be rebuilt in Jerusalem. This could happen very quickly. And third, the ten lost tribes had to be restored to Israel (Jeremiah 31:7-11). This seemed impossible—until now.

Filmmaker Simcha Jacobovici, a traditional Jew, read about the locations where the lost tribes were scattered in Isaiah 11:11. He set up a scientific expedition to find and document the existence of these tribes. Not only did he find them exactly where God scattered them, but he discovered that they had not assimilated!

For example, he found descendants from the tribe of Manasseh living in northeast India. They observe the Sabbath, the festivals, and biblical Jewish laws. In 2000, the Israeli Ministry of the Interior granted citizenship to the first 100 members of the tribe.

All ten "lost" tribes have been located. However, they say, "We are not lost!" Many of the tribes practice an aberrant form of Judaism, but all have relics and customs proving their heritage. I agree with them and the Word of God—they are not lost![1]

Everlasting Covenant of Love

God loves Israel. In Romans 11:28-29, Paul states:

> Concerning the gospel [the Jewish people] are enemies for your sake [so Gentiles can be saved], but concerning the election they are beloved for the sake of the fathers. For the gifts and the calling of

God are irrevocable.

Feel God's covenant love for the Jewish people in Hosea 11:1-4,8:

"When Israel was a child, I loved him.... They sacrificed to the Baals, and burned incense to carved images. I [God] taught Ephraim [Israel] to walk, taking them by their arms...I drew them with gentle cords with bands of love.... I stooped and fed them.... How can I give you up, Ephraim?... My heart churns within Me."

God is crying out to Israel,

"Return, O backsliding children...for I am married to you; I will...bring you to Zion [Israel]" (Jeremiah 3:14).

If God refuses to violate His covenant love for His ancient Jewish people even in the face of their disobedience, imagine the love He has for His New Covenant people. Gentile Christian, stop and contemplate how much God loves you. God says to the older brother (type of Gentile believer) in the parable of the prodigal son: "All that I have is yours" (Luke 15:31b).

The Last Lap

No Jews Allowed

Throughout history, people like Haman in the Book of Esther, Queen Isabella of Spain, and Hitler have cursed the Jew. Entire nations have come against the Jewish people. Even here in "the land of the free," as a young child I remember a sign at the beach that read, "No Dogs or Blacks or Jews Allowed!" (except it used a different word for "Blacks").

What is the result of all these curses? Jewish people as a whole are blind to the Gospel. The devil has backed the Jew into a corner. We have bitterness, pain and hatred in our heart. Our response is understandable. First, we blame God for the Holocaust. Then we blame Christians for our persecution—many church leaders were among those who cursed us (see chapter two). Even for Jews who love God, these wounds are buried deep in our psyche.

How then can believers reach the Jewish people with the Gospel? One of the best methods is with a miracle of physical healing. But there is an even greater way. Malachi 4:5-6 says Elijah will prepare the way for the Messiah. The Spirit that was on Elijah will come on the church and allow it to walk in the pure love of God. Many spiritual "fathers" will be raised up. Their job will be to reveal the love of the Heavenly Father to the world, to the Jew first. Only the compassion of Father God will melt the deep bitterness in Jewish hearts.

Standing with the Jews

The Jews are the most love-starved people on the face of the earth: abused, misunderstood, persecuted, discriminated against, and murdered. We have a covenant with God, but most Jews do not know Him. As a result, many of my people are on the forefront of unbiblical positions such as pro-abortion, pro-homosexual rights, pro-New Age and against school prayer. Some are involved in the smut of Hollywood and even the movement toward a global government. Although we are few percentage-wise, we are disproportionately involved in these causes. (For the sake of fairness, many Jewish people have made scientific and medical discoveries that have brought great benefit to mankind.)

The devil's strategy is to use the anti-God stances of some Jews to cause nominal Christians to join non-believers in hating all Jews. The world and *nominal* Christians will also hate true believers. First they will hate them for standing with the Jew. Then they will hate them for standing with the Jewish Messiah. First the natural, then the spiritual. Christians need to heed the warning Mordecai gave Esther:

"Do not think in your heart that you will escape in the king's palace any more than all the other Jews. For if you remain silent at this time, relief and deliverance will arise for the Jews from another place, but you and your father's house will perish" (Esther 4:13b,14).

If God is for you, who can be against you? God has faith in you. He is passionately and patiently waiting for this last generation to demonstrate Isaiah 49:22-23:

Thus says the Lord GOD: "Behold, I will lift My hand in an oath to the nations [Gentiles], and set up My standard for the peoples; they shall bring your sons [Jewish people] in their arms, and your daughters shall be carried on their shoulders; kings shall be your foster fathers, and their queens your nursing mothers; they shall bow down to you with their faces to the earth, and lick up the dust of your feet. Then you shall know that I am the LORD."

Jewish people will know Yeshua is the Messiah when believers start acting like disciples and stop conforming to the world. The world will hate you, but the multitudes that are in heaven because of you will cheer at your homecoming.

---

[1]The *Quest for the Lost Tribes* video is available from Messianic Vision for $28, postage paid.

8

The One New Man Glorious Congregation

What is the only Bible the first church had? The Old Testament, or as Jewish people would say, the Tenach. What was the last book in that Bible? Although Malachi is the last book in the Christian Old Testament, 2 Chronicles is the last book in the Tenach because the Tenach presents the books of Scripture in a different order. The last words in the Tenach must have great prophetic significance.

In 2 Chronicles 36:23 Cyrus, the Persian king, says, "And [God] has commanded me to build Him a house [temple] at Jerusalem which is in Judah." The spiritual fulfillment of these words will reach its highest expression in the One New Man Congregation of Jew and Gentile.

God says we are to "build Him a temple." His objective is to "gather together in **one** all things in [Messiah]" (Ephesians 1:10). How will He do this?

> "For He Himself is our peace who has made both [Jew and Gentile] **one,** and has broken down the middle wall of division...to create in Himself **one new man**...in whom you also are being built together for a **habitation [dwelling]** of God in the Spirit" (Ephesians 2:14-15,22).

When the wall between Jew and Gentile is removed, the spiritual temple, God's dwelling place, will be restored and this One New Man will release resurrection power to the church that Paul calls "life from the dead" (Romans 11:15)!

How can the devil stop the explosion of God's power? *Stop the building of the temple.* If the foundation is destroyed, the temple can't be built. What is the strategy? Stop Jews from becoming "one" with Gentiles.

The Tabernacle of David
The "tabernacle of David" prophesied by Amos is a type of the One New Man Glorious Congregation:

"On that day I will raise up the tabernacle [literally, 'booth' or figuratively, 'body'] of David [type of Messiah], which has fallen down, and repair its damages; I will raise up its ruins, and rebuild it as in the days of old; that they may possess the remnant of Edom [Septuagint reads 'mankind'], and all the Gentiles who are called by My name," says the LORD who does this thing (Amos 9:11-12).

The tabernacle of David was a unique temple. There was no separation between the people and God. There was no "Holy of Holies." All experienced God's presence. Daily praise was instituted by David before the Lord (1 Chronicles 16:37). The Levites worshiped God with the songs of David set to music.

God promised that once this tabernacle of David was restored it would cause a revival among the Gentiles (Amos 9:12). In fact, this was the proof text to convince the apostles at the Jerusalem Council meeting to evangelize the Gentiles (Acts 15:16-17).

What will cause the release of the flood of God's Spirit? According to Joel 3:18, a fountain will be released "from the house of the LORD." Amos 9:13 says the blessings of revival will be so great that the reaper will not be able to gather all the harvest before the next planting season begins. The plowman will overtake the reaper.

The Last Lap

If Gentiles were the missing part of the church at the time of the Jerusalem Council meeting of Acts 15, who is missing now? After Yeshua died, the veil of the temple was torn in two (Matthew 27:51). Now nothing should separate us from intimacy with God. Yet, the middle wall of division (veil) between Jews and Gentiles hinders the church from achieving its full destiny in God (Ephesians 2:14).

Do You Want to See His Face?

Moses saw God's glory, but could not look at His face.

> And [Moses] said, "Please, show me Your glory."... But He said, "You cannot see My face; for no man shall see Me, and live" (Exodus 33:18,20).

The glory was so intense on Moses after being in God's presence that he had to wear a veil or the brightness would blind the people who looked at him as though they were gazing directly into the sun.

The glory of the Old Covenant tabernacle was so thick that, at times, Moses could not even enter (Exodus 40:35). When the cloud of God's glory filled Solomon's Temple, the priests could not stand (2 Chronicles 5:14). Under the New Covenant, our bodies are the temple of the Holy Spirit (1 Corinthians 6:19). If the Old Covenant glory was so strong, how much greater glory will fill our New Covenant temples when Jew and Gentile become One New Man in Yeshua!

When will this happen? Psalm 102:13-16 states:

"You will arise and have mercy on Zion; for the time to favor her, yes, the set time, has come. For Your servants take pleasure in her stones, and show favor to her dust. So the nations shall fear the name of the LORD, and all the kings of the earth Your glory. For the LORD shall build up Zion; He shall appear in His glory."

When the servants, the Jewish people, take pleasure in (or return to) Israel, the Lord will build up Zion (Jerusalem). When the Lord builds up Zion, He will appear in His glory. This prophecy was written for "the generation to come" (v. 18). The Hebrew could be translated, "for the *last* generation."

This last generation will be uniquely created to restore Davidic praise and worship in order to prepare a tabernacle for the King. As magnificent Levitical worship is restored, it will bring an outpouring of the same glory that was in Solomon's Temple. The Old Covenant glory is the former rain. When the former rain teams up with the latter rain, or the New Covenant glory, we will experience a move of God like the world has never seen.

Miracles in Kiev

The closest to this outpouring I have experienced to date is in the world's largest Messianic Jewish congregation in Kiev, Ukraine. The leader, Rabbi Boris, is almost always in the Spirit where he receives direction from God. When he implements these instructions, the congregation flourishes. What is Boris' secret? He has surrendered to the Holy Spirit.

Over 1,000 Jews and Gentiles gather to worship every Saturday in Boris' congregation. There are normally at least 100 instant healings in *every* service. God instructed Boris to use old-style Chassidic (Orthodox Jewish) worship. The music and dancing are so infectious that almost everyone joins in.

Music usually precedes the move of God. The music that will usher in the One New Man will be a brand new song. It will be the same music described in Revelation 13:3—the song of Moses (Jew) and the song of the Lamb (Christian) becoming one.

It will be a love song from the Bride to her heavenly Bridegroom, from the church to Yeshua. Eye has not seen and ear has not heard what will happen as the Bride and Bridegroom increase in intimacy.

Have you ever been to a Jewish wedding? As great as they are on earth, I want to invite you to the best one ever. You have a golden invitation to the Marriage Supper of the Lamb. There are no regrets allowed.

There is So Much More

As we move toward a One New Man Congregation, the church owes a debt of gratitude to the Messianic Jewish movement. God used this rag-tag army of young Jewish believers in the 1970s to restore the Jewish roots of our faith.

I was less than two years old in the Lord when God put me with an amazing team of Paul Lieberman, Sandra Sheskin Brotman and Marc Sircus (my brother-in-law) to pioneer a Messianic Jewish congregation.

It was God's mercy we survived. In our immaturity, we overacted in our Jewishness. We were resisted and misunderstood by the Gentile church. Both traditional Jews *and* Christians viewed us as a cult.

Initially we only allowed Jews to be in leadership. We didn't use the term "elder" because it sounded too Christian. We didn't allow crosses or pictures of Yeshua in our congregation. The motivation was honorable. We thought that the more Jewish we appeared the more acceptable we would be to the Jewish community. But we didn't reach traditional Jews.

My personal motive for wanting a Messianic Jewish congregation was for my Orthodox Jewish father's salvation. I would say I was a Messianic Jew and my dad would call me a Christian. I would say our building was a synagogue and he would call it a church. I would say, "Yeshua" and he would say, "Jesus." I had not learned yet that battles are won not by man's might nor by man's spirit but only by God's Spirit.

Unintentionally, as we tried to reach traditional Jews, we made Gentile believers who loved us feel like second-class citizens. We had good intentions, but our stance was unbiblical and this I regret.

Over the years I noticed two trends. The majority of the members of Messianic synagogues were Gentiles and the majority of the Jewish people we reached were originally saved in Gentile churches not in Messianic Jewish congregations. Why were so many Gentiles attracted to Messianic Jewish services? Perhaps God had something more in mind for the church?

Much has changed and improved for the better in Messianic Judaism. Without it there would not be One New Man. And it brought a necessary course correction for the church. But God is up to something new. It's bigger than Messianic Judaism. It's bigger than Gentile Christianity. Both have been used mightily by God. But there's more. There's so much more!

9

The Law of Evangelism

One rainy day in Rockville, Maryland, I decided to visit the Judaic library at the Jewish Community Center. A book on the Jews of China caught my eye. It showed pictures of Chinese Jews from Kaifeng, whose ancestors had come to China many generations earlier. They came as silk merchants and lived in cities that made up the "Silk Route." I also noted the reference to Isaiah 49:12, "Surely these shall come from afar; look! those from the north and the west, and these from the land of *Sinim*." The author said Sinim is Hebrew for China. *Imagine*, I thought, *God predicted there would be Jews in China.* I had never even heard of a Chinese Jew. Further, God said they would return to Israel in the last days.

The Last Lap

In 1995 Messianic Jewish evangelist Bob Weiner told the local church I attended that revival had started in China. Pastor Bill Ligon asked if I wanted to team up with him to take a tour group there. I immediately said, "Yes, if we can go to Kaifeng." My motivation in going to Kaifeng was the Law of Evangelism. I knew if we reached out to the Jew, God would bless our efforts to reach all people.

In Kaifeng I met a Chinese Jew who took me to his family cemetery. He proudly showed me twelve generations of his Jewish ancestors. Another Chinese Jew told me, "I am a Jew. I told my son he is a Jew and he must live in Israel!" This man knew nothing about Judaism or Christianity. How could he know that thousands of years earlier God had recorded in the Bible that Jews from China would return to Israel? Since that time he and his entire family have immigrated to Israel.

As part of the tour, we brought singers and dancers to Kaifeng to conduct a Feast of Tabernacles celebration. This event was televised throughout the *entire city*. When we went to the Jew first, God opened up a door to reach the whole area.

Don't Compromise

A best-selling Christian author has written a book saying that it is unbiblical to "go to the Jew first" with the

Gospel. He argues that Jewish people have suffered so much they should not be targeted for evangelism by overzealous Christians. A well-meaning Christian who reads this will feel there is no need to evangelize the Jew. Many believers who say they love the Jewish people and Israel share this *anti-Semitic* thinking. I'm sure they genuinely love the Jew and Israel, but they need to realize that the most *anti-Semitic* act is *not* to share the Gospel. They must be careful not to value their relationship with the Jewish community more highly than obedience to God's Word.

It is true that after all these centuries of persecution by so-called "Christians," we *must* love the Jew. Only acts of "supernatural love" will melt the centuries of misunderstandings. But don't fall into the trap of a love without Yeshua.

May the words of Ezekiel 3:17-18 and Acts 4:12 ring in our ears:

"Son of man, I have made you a watchman **for the house of Israel;**… When I say to the wicked, 'You shall surely die,' and you give him no warning…his blood I will require at your hand."

"Nor is there salvation in any other, for there is no other name under heaven given among men by which we must be saved."

The Last Lap

Follow the Pattern

The Law of Evangelism is found in Romans 1:16:

> "For I am not ashamed of the gospel of [Messiah], for it is the power of God to salvation for everyone who believes, for the Jew first...."

This was God's *historical* order to reach the world. But it is *also* God's *spiritual* order.

This pattern is found throughout Scripture. When Yeshua went to the Jew first, it opened up a supernatural door of evangelism for all people. Yeshua commanded His disciples, "Go rather to the lost sheep of the house of Israel" (Matthew 10:6). The Messiah realized that by planting a seed to the "Jew first," it would open up the world. Since the Jewish people have been spread to the four corners of the earth (Isaiah 11:12), when you go to the Jews, you reach virtually everyone else too.

The principle that causes the Law of Evangelism to operate is found in Genesis 12:3. God promises to bless those who bless the Jewish people. As we sow seed into the Jewish people by sharing with them the Good News, we will in turn reap an abundant harvest among the Gentiles.

This amazing truth of going to the Jew first was known by John Owen, one of the greatest Puritan theologians. He said, "There is not any promise anywhere of raising up a kingdom unto the Lord Jesus Christ in this world but it is either expressed, or clearly intimated, that the beginning of it must be with the Jews."[1]

God says He will pour out His Spirit on all flesh in the last days. As a result, Jewish sons and daughters will prophesy (Joel 2:28). The Jewish people will experience a major revival. The prophet Joel says this will happen at the time the nations try to partition Israel (3:2). And it will be the catalyst for the greatest revival in history. Zechariah says:

"Thus says the Lord of hosts: 'In those days ten men from every language of the nations shall grasp the sleeve [fringes of the prayer shawl] of a Jewish man, saying, "Let us go with you, for we have heard that God is with you"'" (Zechariah 8:23).

God will cause His former rain (Spirit of God on the Jewish people) and His latter rain (Spirit of God on Christians) to come down at *once* (Joel 2:23). Rain brings life for harvest. This specific miracle has never happened in history. The supernatural downpour of the two rains simultaneously will birth the One New Man Glorious Congregation resulting in multitudes being saved!

The Last Lap

---

[1]John Owen quoted in *A Puritan Golden Treasury*, compiled by I. D. E. Thomas (Carlisle, PA: Banner of Truth, 1977) pp. 155, 157 as cited in Michael Brown, *Our Hands Are Stained with Blood* (Shippensburg, PA: Destiny Image, 1992), p. 20.

10

You and Your House

When I tell believers they need to reach the Jewish people with the Gospel, some are exasperated. "But Sid," they protest, "I have tried to share Yeshua with Jewish people. They are just not interested."

This is God's appointed time to reach Israel. But it can't be done by man's methods. I'm an expert on how it *can't* be done. I have tried just about everything. Although most of these methods have worked to some degree, the revival prophesied in Joel 2:28 has not fully manifested. If it is God's time to reach Jewish people with the Gospel and to form the One New Man Glorious Congregation, then how will it take place?

God has given me a prophetic example through my father. When I accepted the Lord, he was shocked, outraged, and embarrassed. My dad was born in Poland into a traditional Jewish family. To say the least, he was not raised to love Christianity. He told me that when he was a young boy, his father would spit at a church as they walked past. Whenever I talked about Yeshua, the conversation ended in shouting, anger, and much hurt. My public, vocal witness for Yeshua brought him shame.

My mother was another story. She was also Jewish, but was born in America. Although she attended the traditional synagogue to please my father, she was not as fervent. When I accepted the Lord, she wasn't happy, but never let it interfere with her love for me. She was grateful that my experience with God had restored my marriage and made me a far more responsible person.

While my mom tolerated my beliefs, she was not quick to follow them. When I shared prophecies that proved Yeshua was the Jewish Messiah, it didn't faze her. When I prayed for her and others and they were healed, it interested her, but didn't change her. Finally, as she observed the peace and fulfillment I had over many years, the Lord broke through and she received Him.

Immediately after I had my experience with Yeshua, I began to share my testimony. Wherever I spoke I asked people to pray for my father's salvation. My mother was not so hopeful. She would sigh and tell me, "Your father will never believe in Jesus!"

I replied without the slightest doubt, "I *know* he will become a believer." From that point on I began to say often, "I *know* my father will become a believer." I said it so many times, I began to believe it.

My mother didn't want me to be disappointed. She was sure it was impossible for a Jewish person like my father to believe. But Yeshua says in Mark 9:23, "If you can believe, **all** things are possible." And I had long since moved from hope to faith.

After Mom died, my father asked me to go to the synagogue for a year and say a memorial prayer (Kaddish) for her. I knew it would not do her any good. She was already in heaven. But for my father's sake I went. Many people at the synagogue who did not like that I was an outspoken believer, still told my father I was a good son for going every day to the synagogue. After that year my dad had many close calls with death. I remember telling people, "Dad can't die. He hasn't received Yeshua yet."

But then I got the call from my sister, Shirley. My father was dying. Shirley and her husband Marc had been believers in the Messiah almost as long as I had. "It looks bad," Shirley told me, "You'd better come." Without hesitation, I booked a flight.

Something unusual had happened to me a week earlier. A tangible, wonderful peace from God had come all over my body. This had happened before, but it was different this time. It stayed with me twenty-four hours a day and it was getting stronger. I didn't know the reason for it, but I was grateful.

When I arrived, I met my sister at the hospital and we went straight to intensive care. My dad was 83 and had prostate cancer. Since the cancer had invaded his bones we knew he could die at any moment. His voice was so weak he could barely speak above a whisper. I asked, "Dad, don't you want to be in the same place as Mom? She used to say, 'Heaven must be such a wonderful place.' Do you want to make Yeshua your Messiah and Lord?"

He replied, "Yes," and we prayed.

Then my sister said, "Sid, I didn't hear him."

I responded, "Shirley, that was *good* for Dad. *I* heard him."

She put her hands on her hips and said, "I'm not sure. Dad, do you want to make Yeshua your Messiah and Lord?"

My father got his old spunk back and belted out, "Yes!"

With that Shirley began to jump up and down and scream very loudly, "Thank you, Yeshua! Thank you!" My sister was a conservative schoolteacher. This was totally out of character for her. Besides, in the intensive care ward everyone is supposed to remain very quiet. I tried to calm her down—to no avail. She said, "I promised the Lord, I would jump for joy when Dad was saved!"

My father went to heaven the next day.

The Anointing Destroys the Yoke
Many have witnessed to Jewish people without any visible signs of success. As a result, they have stopped witnessing. But we are in a new season. It is the set time to favor Zion. God must restore the Jewish branches to the olive tree. We cannot have the "Glorious Church" until the middle wall of separation comes down between Jew and Gentile to birth the One New Man. God is once again having mercy on Israel.

How was my father saved? Remember the anointing that came upon me a week before he died? "And the yoke will be destroyed because of the anointing..." (Isaiah 10:27). The anointing of the Holy Spirit destroys the demonic yokes of unbelief. Get ready for the anointing for Jewish evangelism that is being poured out. All things are possible to those who believe. If a Jew like my father can be saved, so can the Jewish person whom God will have cross your path! It's "not by might nor by power, but by My Spirit, says the LORD of hosts" (Zechariah 4:6b).

The Last Lap

A Lamb for a House

I am blessed because my entire family knows Yeshua. But this is God's norm. In the book of Exodus, God says the lamb sacrificed at Passover is for the *entire* household (12:3). All of Noah's household was saved from the worldwide flood. The scarlet cord, which represents the blood, protected Rahab's entire family from being killed (Joshua 2:18). Joshua knew the heart of God for families to be saved when he said, "But as for me and **my house,** we will serve the LORD" (Joshua 24:15b). When Cornelius, a Gentile, came to accept Yeshua as Savior, it resulted in his whole family being saved as well (Acts 10:24,44). In Acts 16:31 Paul said to the Philippian jailer, "Believe on the Lord [Yeshua the Messiah], and you will be saved, **you and your household."**

The Jewish law for family evangelism applies not just to one member of a household, but the entire mishpochah (family). You *and your house* will be saved! A lamb for a house!

11

Christian Telephone

M any years ago I heard about a unique tradition at an Orthodox synagogue in Washington, D.C. Whenever someone went to the platform to read from the Torah, he would bend his knees and lower his head about a foot then stand back up before he got to the Torah scroll. Many years later a curious member asked, "Rabbi, why do we dip so low before reading the Torah?" The rabbi explained that the synagogue had previously been located in the basement of another building. Just in front of the Torah was a low water pipe. The only way to get to the Scriptures without hitting your head was to dip low.

As a Jew, I have experienced enough tradition to last a lifetime. But Christianity is loaded with tradition as well. It's a human problem. We all have patterns with which we feel most comfortable. A pastor feels he has to accommodate all these comfort zones. If he is unsuccessful, he often burns out or quits. If he succeeds, the spiritual development of the church is hindered.

Religious groups that have been around the longest have the most tradition. For instance, we Jewish people have more tradition than the Catholics. The Catholics have more tradition than the Protestants. Pentecostals have more tradition than the Charismatics who, in turn, have more tradition than the Word of Faith movement. You get the idea. After going to a specific church for many years, tradition sets in. You find yourself uncomfortable in other expressions in the Body of Messiah.

What would happen if the church that always wears choir robes suddenly cast them aside? What if the drums, bass, and guitar were to get very loud in a traditional service? How about the pastor showing up with no tie or suit on a Sunday morning? Before you poke fun because you attend a church where the members only wear T-shirts and jeans, how would you react if your pastor showed up in a suit and tie?

What if there was no "special" music before the pastor spoke? Or what if the pastor suddenly started shaking under the power of God and others began wailing and travailing in the Spirit? What if a mighty wind with flames of fire came into your church building and people started speaking in tongues and acting like they were drunk (Acts 2:1-15)?

What would happen if our congregations were more "God sensitive" than "seeker sensitive"? What is more important—God showing up, or your traditional order of service?

If the pastor yields to the Spirit, he will immediately start a membership drive—he will drive the members who are preventing revival right out of his church. Some members will say, "I have been a believer for thirty years and God has never worked that way." Others will be uncomfortable because the pastor is preaching the Lordship of Yeshua—not a watered down version of a cheap life insurance policy. It will not be two hymns and a hum and out by noon. The entertainment mode will be gone forever, may it rest in peace.

On occasion the pastor might be so caught up into worship a service could end without him bringing something from the Word. Members might be forced to experience the "Living Word." Children and teenagers will not be shipped out to watch videos. They will all be at the front of the church weeping for the lost.

The Last Lap

Back to Basics

Did you ever play the game of "telephone" as a child? One person whispers a phrase into another person's ear. By the time the message passes through several people, it is completely distorted. This is what has happened in the church. We have wandered from the old paths. We need a more far reaching reformation than the one started by Martin Luther. We need to return to the God of our fathers. All the way back.

The early church met in houses. Acts 2:46 says, they were "breaking bread from house to house." Everyone participated at these house meetings. "Whenever you come together, **each of you** has a psalm, has a teaching, has a tongue, has a revelation, has an interpretation" (1 Corinthians 14:26). How is this possible in a large meeting? It's not.

In many churches today, members slip through the cracks without the pastor even knowing. We expect a pastor to be a great administrator, fund raiser, builder, speaker, prophet, evangelist, apostle, teacher, and worship leader. Is this what God intended?

The root meaning of the word "pastor" is "to protect," from which we get the term, "shepherd." When Yeshua prayed for more laborers for the harvest in Matthew 9:38, He was talking about shepherds (v. 36). A shepherd opens up his or her heart to comfort, teach, protect, and love the sheep. An ideal place to do this is in home meetings like the early church.

The emphasis in these meetings will not be on the "one man show," but on the "One New Man Body." The people will really get to know one another. They will become "mishpochah" (Hebrew for "family") by sharing meals and demonstrating God's Kingdom on earth.

Because people will become *participants* rather than *spectators* the groups will grow in leadership and gifting. These smaller meetings will restore the Jewish mindset as opposed to the Greco-Roman approach. The biblical Jewish way is worshiping and acknowledging God and placing Him first in a total commitment, twenty-four hours a day, seven days a week. The Greco-Roman perspective is worshiping or acknowledging God only at certain times.

Miracles will become common in home groups that are yielded to God's Spirit. Because of the love and unity within the group, believers will be added continually. Everyone will be a productive, functioning member.

The successful home meeting will burst out of the walls. This will be their sign to start another group, not to build a "Golden Cathedral." With blessings they will send one family out to open their home for a new house meeting.

The house groups can come together for special services. These corporate meetings can be for worship, teaching, discipleship, evangelism, and celebrating the biblical festivals. However, the goal of the small groups will not be to add members to a "mother church," but to function as part of the Body of Messiah and to add members to the Body.

New Wineskins

Could it be when we rejected the Jewish roots of our faith, we lost our first love? We abandoned the biblical festivals in favor of holidays mixed with paganism. We substituted an "emperor" or "king" system of church government for God's system. Things got so complex we needed a seminary education to run the business of church. We replaced participating members of the One Body of Messiah with spectators. We needed so much money for the bricks and mortar and overhead we had to rely on the secular government to feed widows and orphans.

How will the restoration begin? It will start as the result of national judgments from God. This will cause the pastors in a city to seek so much after God they will forget about the walls that divide them and begin to seek God together. This supernatural unity of repentance and calling out to God for revival will bring a new wave of God's Spirit. It will be different than anything we have ever experienced. It will be a spiritual tidal wave.

After the pastors come together, there will also be a supernatural unity among the congregations. They will be further united by observing the biblical festivals together. These celebrations will bring the greatest outpouring of joy and God's Spirit in history.

Many in the church today feel a godly discontent. We know the old manna doesn't taste good any longer. We are crying out for something more. We hunger for greater intimacy with God. Our old wineskins cannot contain the glory that is coming to the church.

Lord, you know I don't have all the answers. But You love Your church. Please restore to us the joy of our salvation. Give us the grace to sell out to Your Kingdom. Give us the courage to scrap the man-made foundations in order to be able to contain the glory of the One New Man anointing. Show us what it means to put on the One New Man (Ephesians 4:24).

12

Are You Ready?

Why does the Word of God command us to pray for the peace of Jerusalem? It doesn't say pray for the peace of Washington, D.C.; Paris; London; or Berlin; only Jerusalem. It is so important to God that He promises great blessings for those who pray. "Pray for the peace of Jerusalem: 'may they **prosper** who love you'" (Psalm 122:6). The word "prosper" refers to something more important than money. In Hebrew it means, "heart peace."

Jerusalem means "City of Peace." One day soon Yeshua will rule Jerusalem and the Word of the Lord will be broadcast from that city to the whole world (Isaiah 2:1-4). When we pray for the peace of Jerusalem, we are praying for the return of Messiah

The Last Lap

Yeshua. We are praying for Jerusalem to become the true City of Peace. We are praying for worldwide revival. We are praying for curses to come off Jewish people. We are praying for the Jewish people to be saved so the world can believe. We are praying for the completion of the One New Man.

The devil and his crowd are doing everything possible to abort God's plan. Yeshua said He would not return until the Jewish people say, "Blessed is He who comes in the name of the LORD!" (Matthew 23:39). But this does not concern the devil as much as the great harvest that will come when the Jewish branch is grafted back into the olive tree. It will cause the life of God to explode through His One New Man to a dying humanity (Romans 11:15).

Everything is about to come full circle. The first to get the Good News were the Jewish people, but they will also be the last to get the Gospel. Yeshua said, "So the last will be first, and the first last" (Matthew 20:16a). God is about ready to move the Jew and Israel to center stage once again.

It is as though we are watching a video of church history in reverse. The closer we get to the return of the Messiah the more the Body will look like the first church and the focus of the world will be on the Jew and Israel.

The restoration of the Jewish roots of the church is

happening before our eyes. The church will become more Hebraic in culture. Jewish believers will move into leadership in the church, just as it was at first. There also will be a restoration of the temple, both physical and spiritual. And, of course, the Jews are already returning to Israel.

The world will envy the Jew and Israel because of the material blessings God will lavish on her. Before the day of the Lord's judgment occurs, God describes Israel as "like the Garden of Eden" (Joel 2:3). Other nations will invade Israel to acquire its wealth:

> "You will say, 'I will go up against a land of unwalled villages...' to take plunder and to take booty, to stretch out your hand against the waste places that are again inhabited, and against a people gathered from the nations, who have acquired livestock and goods.... 'Have you come to take plunder? Have you gathered your army to take booty, to carry away silver and gold, to take away livestock and goods, to take great plunder?'" (Ezekiel 38:11-13).

Not only will the world be jealous of and hate Israel in that day, but so will the religious, institutional, humanistic part of the church.

Dividing the Sheep from the Goats

The plumbline for the church and the nations is always Israel. Genesis 12:3 is still true where God promises to bless those who bless the Jewish people and curse those who curse them. How much more so at this set time to favor Zion!

God says in Matthew 25:31-46 that nations will be divided as a shepherd separates goats from sheep. A goat has a mind of its own but a sheep follows the shepherd. Yeshua tells us what the dividing line will be: "Assuredly, I say to you, inasmuch as you did it to one of the least of these My brethren [Greek means "from the womb"—the Jewish people], you did it to Me" (Matthew 25:40). The same single judgment issue is mentioned prophetically in Joel 3:2:

> "I will also gather all nations...and **I will enter into judgment** with them there **on account of My people, My heritage Israel,** whom they have scattered among the nations; they have also divided up My land."

The Two-Edged Sword

Many Christians are calling out for the anointing. Multitudes are earnestly praying for the return of the Lord. But Amos 1:2 and 5:18 say:

"The Lord roars from Zion, and utters His voice from Jerusalem; the pastures of the shepherds mourn...." Woe to you who desire the day of the LORD!

Remember Ananias and Sapphira in the book of Acts? They thought God would wink at their secret sins. They thought wrong. The anointing did not bring a blessing. It brought destruction. The glory of God will be a two-edged sword. For those who make Yeshua Lord of all, it will be the greatest blessing of their life. But for those who are lukewarm or make Yeshua their religious life insurance policy, it will be the worst moment of their life.

There will be two types of churches operating at the same time. They are like the last two churches mentioned in the book of Revelation—the church in Philadelphia and the church of the Laodiceans. Those of the church of Philadelphia will have God's name written on them indicating intimacy with Him. They will be totally surrendered to God. They will have the key of David to unlock the heart of the Jew.

The others will be lukewarm like the church of Laodicea. God will vomit them out of His mouth (Revelation 3:16). The warning: You must be red-hot for Yeshua. If you are a goat in reference to the Jew and Israel, Yeshua will say, "Depart from Me, you cursed, into the everlasting fire prepared for the devil and his angels..." (Matthew 25:41). Will you be an authentic Philadelphian church believer, or a counterfeit Laodicean church member?

13

The Double River

God is preparing to release His champion, His One New Man, for the last lap. But first the wineskins must be changed to contain the outpouring of His Spirit.

Could We Do Another Show?

I recently experienced the anointing that will enable this change. I was taping my television show with a very nervous guest. He had two big reference books and about fifty charts. Since we do not have a table on the set, he had to hold all these props in his lap.

This would never do. I gently said he would have to set aside his materials. We could put his charts in later when we edited the show. Reluctantly, he gave up his security blanket.

After we recorded a few minutes of the program, it became clear it just wasn't going to work. My producer came onto the set to remind me we were under a deadline. She suggested we go on to another show and move this one to the end of the day. In other words, if we ran out of time we could scrap this program. I quickly agreed.

My last guest before coming back to the nervous guest, said during a commercial break, "Do you feel that? I'm getting drunk in the Spirit." I felt the same outpouring of God's Spirit that he was feeling. And for the first time in my life I started getting drunk in the Spirit too. It was wonderful.

No high from drugs or alcohol could compare. I'm sure this was how the first Jewish believers in Yeshua felt when the Holy Spirit came upon them at Shavuot (Pentecost). Remember, they were accused of being drunk (Acts 2:13). It was like the anointing I received when my father got saved. It was the same anointing that released miracles in Ukraine under Rabbi Boris.

When it came time to try again with the nervous guest, I felt so good I wasn't even expecting any problems. In the natural a drunk doesn't worry about anything. He is completely transparent and will say whatever comes to mind. He has no fear or inhibitions. In the supernatural when you are drunk in the Spirit, you surrender completely to God. You hear God's voice more clearly and nothing gets in the way of your obedience. All stress disappears.

Before I knew it, we had completed the program. I was so free, it caused my guest to relax. It turned out to be wonderful. We had such a good time, he asked me right after we finished, "Could we do another show?"

I know a pastor who was drunk in the Holy Spirit for two weeks. By the time he came to his natural senses the revival in his congregation was up and running.

The Missing Ingredient

If the healing revival of the 1950s could have ushered in the One New Man, it would have happened. If the Messianic Jewish and the Charismatic movements of the 1970s could have ushered in the One New Man, it would have happened. If the Word of Faith movement in the 1980s could have ushered in the One New Man, it would have happened.

If the renewal and revival movement of the 1990s could have ushered in the One New Man, it would have happened. If the restoration of the five-fold ministry in the late 1990s could have ushered in the One New Man, it would have happened. If the restoration of holiness and worship and all-night prayer and fasting could have ushered in the One New Man, it would have happened. Although these are important ingredients, they haven't produced the One New Man.

What is the missing ingredient to trigger the flood of God's Spirit as described in Ezekiel 47? God says, "And wherever the **double** river shall go...everything shall live" (Ezekiel 47:9, Amp.). This river will cause everything it touches to be made whole. Sickness will not be able to exist in this *double* river. It will be so deep we will sink unless we are one-hundred percent dependent on God.

Why does God call it a double river? Ezekiel 37 says the breath of God will blow on the dead bones of the house of Israel and they will live. When revival hits the Jewish people, it will breathe life into the lukewarm Gentile church as well (Romans 11:15).

The *double* river is a picture of the unity of Jew and Gentile. The principle of double river unity is also illustrated in Ezekiel 37:19. The two sticks in that verse are identified in the text as Israel (the Northern Kingdom) and Judah (the Southern Kingdom). The Lord says, concerning these two sticks, that He will make them "one stick" in His hand. Even so the Lord will also make Jewish and Gentile believers one in Him, producing in the One New Man an anointing greater than the sum of the parts.

Now you can understand David's prayer in Psalm 133:

Behold, how good and how pleasant it is for brethren to dwell together in **unity!** It is like the precious oil [Holy Spirit] upon the head, running down on the beard, the beard of Aaron, running down on the edge of his garments. It is like the dew of Hermon, descending upon the mountains of Zion; for there the LORD **commanded the blessing**—life forevermore.

The blessings of God will be released when the unity of the Jew and Gentile form One New Man.

The Esther Anointing

The pattern for the end-time Glorious Church is found in the book of Esther. Esther was a beautiful, pure virgin who had favor with man and the king. Esther also hid her Jewish roots.

For six months, Esther (whom we can view as a type of the church) soaked in the oil of myrrh. The myrrh plant is bitter on the outside. But when it is crushed, it releases the sweet fragrance within. Crushing makes you bitter or better. Then Esther soaked six months in perfumes to prepare her to meet the king. The soaking in perfume represents dwelling in the manifest presence of God, the anointing, followed by intense repentance, prayer, and fasting.

The devil's strategy was to murder *all* the Jewish

people. Satan knew if he could destroy the Jew he could prevent the coming of the Messiah. And he has tried to destroy the Jew after Yeshua came because he understands the significance of the One New Man. Without the Jew there would be no One New Man.

Queen Esther was the *only* one who could go to the king to save the Jewish people. She could have just enjoyed her life of royalty without taking any risks. Some in the church today continue to soak in the anointing and do nothing.

Esther knew it was life-threatening to reveal her Jewish connection. But it would have been more dangerous to keep quiet. Mordecai warned Esther: "Do not think in your heart that you will escape in the king's palace any more than all the other Jews" (Esther 4:13b). Some Gentiles might think anti-Semitism doesn't affect them. But after the devil turns against the Jew, he will come after the Christian.

> "For if you remain completely silent at this time, relief and deliverance will arise for the Jews from another place, but you and your father's house will perish. Yet who knows whether you have come to the kingdom for such a time as this?" (Esther 4:14).

When Esther stood up for the Jewish people, they were saved and revival broke out among the Gentiles

(Esther 8:17). I pray in Yeshua's name that you receive the same anointing that was on Queen Esther. Take a moment and receive the Esther anointing.

Many are in the crushing stage. "Weeping may endure for a night, but joy comes in the morning" (Psalm 30:5b). In the morning comes the soaking in perfume, the anointing. Then comes intimacy with the King of Kings which results in radical, passionate believers who instantly follow His command and identify with their biblical roots and stand up for the Jewish people.

Following that will be worldwide revival. We will flow in love, power, compassion, and the miraculous. People will literally see flames of fire coming from us (Hebrews 1:7b). It will be natural for all sold-out believers to preach the Gospel.

Although I have presented many of the ingredients of the One New Man Congregation, it will include much more. The one thing for sure is that the next, greatest, and last move of God's Spirit will be different from anything any of us has ever seen.

Please, please, please do not use this book as a cookie cutter to create a new denomination. If I have learned anything about God, it is that He is bigger than our boxes. Some One New Man Congregations will be mega churches and some will have only one home group of five people. Some will be very biblically

The Last Lap

Jewish in culture and others will only celebrate the biblical festivals. Let God be God.

Be ready for change. The Bride will take on a whole new appearance. She will have some characteristics of Messianic Judaism and some of Gentile Christianity. But this I know, Yeshua will feel very much at home.

Appendix A

Is the Church the "New Israel"?
Replacement Theology Biblically Analyzed

by Keith Parker

T he idea that the Church is the "new" Israel is by no means a modern phenomenon, but it has recently made a comeback, particularly in "Restorationist" circles. The doctrine is usually called "Replacement Theology," and means that the Church has finally and forever replaced Israel in the purposes of God.

The Last Lap

The Purpose of this Article:

Our purpose in these pages is to define what the Replacement Doctrine actually says, and to ask whether it is in fact true to the teaching of scripture. We shall ask, and seek to answer, the questions: "Do the Jewish people as such still have any significant place in the plan of God?" "Do God's territorial promises to Israel still stand?" and "Does the modern State of Israel have prophetic significance, or is it an historic accident?"

Extreme View of Some Christians:

At the start, let it be said that the extreme views of some Christian "Israel fanatics" may have provoked understandable cynicism in some Christian quarters. This article does not seek to argue an extreme case, such as that Jews do not need to repent and turn to Jesus their Messiah, or that the policies of the modern State of Israel are always right. We are setting out to explore what the Bible actually teaches concerning Israel.

A Short Definition of the Replacement Doctrine:

1. Israel has been replaced by the Christian Church in the purposes of God, or, more precisely, the Church is the historic continuation of Israel.

2. The Jewish people are therefore no longer "Israel." They are just another people group, like all other nations and religions, who need, and can receive, salvation in Jesus the Messiah.

3. Apart from salvation, and incorporation into the Body of Messiah, the Jews have no future, no hope, and no calling.

4. Since Pentecost, Israel, properly so-called IS the Church.

How Replacement Theologians Argue Their Case:

1. To be a son of Abraham is to have faith in Messiah Jesus. Galatians 3:29 shows that sonship of Abraham is seen in spiritual, not national terms.

2. The promise of Canaan to Abraham was only a "starter." The real promised land is the whole world (Romans 4:13). It will be the Church that inherits the world.

3. The nation of Israel was only the seed of the future Church which would arise, incorporating people of all nations (Malachi 1:11).

The Last Lap

4. Jesus taught that the Jews would lose their spiritual privileges, and be replaced by another people (Matthew 21:43). The question raised by the apostles in Acts 1:6, "Lord, wilt thou at this time restore again the kingdom to Israel?" is ignored by Jesus as unworthy of comment.

5. A true Jew is anyone born of the Spirit, whether he is racially Gentile or Jewish (Romans 2:28-29).

6. Paul shows that the Church was really the same "olive tree" as was Israel. Therefore to distinguish between Israel and the Church is, strictly speaking, false. Indeed, people of Jewish origin need to be grafted back into the Church i.e., into Israel proper (Romans 11:17-23).

7. All the Old Testament promises made to Israel, unless they were historically fulfilled before the first coming of Messiah, are now the property of the Christian Church. They are not to be interpreted carnally and literally, but spiritually and symbolically. Therefore OT references to Israel, Jerusalem, Zion, and the Temple, when they are predictive, refer to the Church (2 Corinthians 1:20). In the NT all these things are understood spiritually (see Galatians 4:21-26; 6:16; Ephesians 2:19-22; Hebrews 12:22).

The Attractions of Replacement Theology:

(a) It is historically well rooted in the Church (Church Fathers, Luther, the Reformers).

(b) It has an intellectual appeal, because it does not require literal interpretation of the Bible.

(c) It has a freshness appeal, because it goes along with a view of the "Last Things" that cuts across the often fanciful end-time teachings, which have been current in the Church (through the influence of the Plymouth Brethren, and the Scofield Bible) over the last century or so.

(d) It appeals to that side of human character, which has difficulty in acceding to the election of others.

Having stated the case, which the Replacement teachers would put forward, let us now consider how other Christians, who believe that the Jews are still special to God, would argue their case.

A General Statement:

(a) To be a son of Abraham is open to all by faith, but physical sonship still exists. Israel (the Jews), have and will have an important place in the purposes of God.

(b) By no means is it true that every Israelite has been, is, or shall be, saved.

(c) *Unlike any other nation,* Israel has been chosen by God for His purposes of redemption for the whole world.

(d) Through Israel the promised Redeemer and Messiah came into the world. *Both the first and second comings* of Jesus are to be on their territory.

(e) Individually, Jews, as well as Gentiles, can only be saved in this age through faith in the person and work of the Messiah, Yeshua (Jesus).

(f) Historically, a large part of the nation (though by no means all, if we are to believe the record of the book of Acts) rejected the true Messiah, and for that reason lost possession of their land, and their destiny as a priestly people *for a season.*

(g) There has, in all the centuries since Jesus the Messiah, been a number of Jews, who came to know and love Jesus, though at the expense of being swallowed up in a Church, which by this time had forgotten its Jewish origins.

(h) *The Jewish people are unique in human history: they retained their identity as a people, despite having no homeland or political structure, despite frequent attempts at genocide and forcible conversion, and despite their own desires to become indistinguishable from their Gentile neighbours.*

(i) God made some very clear promises to the Jews as a people. How could He possibly redefine them to apply to another people without being charged with deviousness?

(j) Since the 1840s there are more Jews believing in Jesus than since the first century.

(k) The State of Israel has been reestablished, though yet in unbelief. It has been so far preserved remarkably, if not miraculously, through many crises. Those who believe in the sovereignty of God within History find in this the marks of Divine Providence.

The Last Lap

(l) *There is yet to be a time when Jews in large numbers will turn to Jesus,* having a strong influence on the evangelization of the Gentile world.

(m) In our day there are *significant and growing congregations of Hebrew-speaking Jews in Israel,* who proclaim Jesus as Messiah and Saviour to their own people. They are not part of any Gentile denominational organization. They bear the marks of a fresh direction in the work of God.

WHAT THE SCRIPTURES SAY ABOUT ISRAEL

1. The general pattern of scripture is that its histories and predictions are literal, though often trimmed with poetic and pictorial language. This allows for the use of "type" and "antitype" in scripture. This can be checked by reference to significant examples of fulfilled predictions in the Bible.

(a) The prophecy about the altar at Bethel. 1 Kings 13:2 gives the prediction and 2 Kings 23:15-17 shows the fulfillment.

(b) Messiah is to be born of a virgin (Isaiah 7:14 and Matthew 1:23).

(c) Messiah will be born in Bethlehem (Micah 5:2). For those who spiritualize the prophecies, it would not have mattered had He been born in Birmingham.

(d) Messiah will ride into Jerusalem on an ass (Zechariah 9:9 and Matthew 21:5).

(e) Messiah will suffer excruciating pain at the hands of men (Psalm 22).

(f) Messiah will be killed, and buried in a rich man's grave (Isaiah 53:8-9).

(g) Messiah will be alive again after His death (Isaiah 53:10).

2. If in the case of fulfilled prophecy the fulfillment is literal, then it is logical to expect unfulfilled prophecies to be literal also.

Thus, when God speaks of Jerusalem, Judah, and Israel in the last days, we can accept this at face value. Jesus, for example, predicted the destruction of the Temple (Matthew 24:2), and that Jerusalem would be dominated by the Gentiles until much later in history (Luke 21:24). How can this be interpreted of the Church? In fact the predictions were fulfilled in AD 70 and 1967. The Bible, of course, also refers to the "heavenly Jerusalem," but there is no difficulty in perceiving when it means the earthly or the heavenly Jerusalem.

3. Meaning of 'Israel' and 'Jew' in the New Testament:

There are about 77 references to "Israel" in the New Testament. One refers to the land of Israel, and every single one of the rest refer to the Jewish people either historically, in their unbelief, or as the believing remnant. The one reference which is debated is Galatians 6:16, where Paul says "as many as walk according to this rule, peace be on them, and mercy, and upon the Israel of God." In view of the fact that the word "Israel" never refers elsewhere in scripture to the Christian Church, it is best to interpret Galatians 6:16 as referring to the body of Jews who believe in Jesus, who are, of course, part of the Church.

The word "Jew" or "Jews" occurs over 190 times in the NT. It always refers to the Jewish people, whether to those who rejected the Messiah, or to those who accepted Him. It is never used to describe a Gentile Christian. Romans 2:28-29, far from *extending* the title of "Jew" to Gentile Christians is actually *restricting* "true Jewishness" to those Jews who are circumcised in heart, i.e., who accept Jesus, and are born of the Spirit.

While insisting that Jews and Gentiles within the Church constitute "one new man" (Ephesians 2:15), and that the spiritual standing of Jews and Gentiles in Messiah is equal (Galatians 3:28; 6:15), Paul did make a practical distinction, not only between men and women, but also between Christians of Jewish and Gentile backgrounds.

This is illustrated by his attitude to his two colleagues, Timothy and Titus; Timothy, who was Jewish, he circumcised (Acts 16:3), but he sternly resisted pressure to circumcise Titus, because he was a Gentile (Galatians 2:3). Paul did not teach that either Jews or Gentiles had a superior position within the ecclesia on grounds of race. This outlaws discrimination against anyone within the Church on ground of his racial origin.

Paul in fact distinguishes between three groups of people in the world: "Jews, Gentiles, and the Church of God" (1 Corinthians 10:32). This means that a Christian has transcended his racial background, though for practical purposes he is still a member of his own nation.

The Last Lap

4. The evidence of the Epistles of James and Peter:
James addresses his epistle to "the twelve tribes in the Diaspora" (literal translation). Clearly he saw the Jewish Christians, to whom he was writing, as still Israelites. He describes their meeting as a "synagogue" (2:2 literal Greek). Peter was given an "apostleship to the circumcision [i.e., to the Jews]" (Galatians 2:8). This is why Peter's first epistle is written from Babylonia, where the largest First Century Jewish community resided (1 Peter 5:13), and was addressed to "chosen exiles of the Diaspora" (1 Peter 1:1 literal Greek).

5. The Teaching of the Apostle Paul:
Paul was a Jew, and also the chosen apostle to the Gentiles. (In fact I cannot find even one non-Jewish apostle in the NT). *Paul's epistle to the Romans is the theological heart of the NT.* Chapters 9-11 contain his mature teaching about Israel. Look now in detail at what he says, and see that Paul does not replace Israel by the Church.

(a) The Jews, even in their rejection of Jesus are *still* Israelites (Romans 9:4).

(b) To Israel *still belong* the adoption, the glory, the *covenants* [including the new covenant], the giving of the law, the service of God, and the *promises* (Romans 9:4).

(c) The main body of Israel has forfeited salvation through rejecting the Messiah (Romans 9:30-33; 10:21).

(d) Paul desires and *prays for their salvation* (Romans 10:1-4). There is no anti-Jewishness in Paul's heart—quite the opposite (Romans 9:1-3).

(e) Israel is *not* finally rejected (Romans 11:1-2). Even in OT times, there was only a remnant of true believers among a nation largely composed of unbelievers. In Paul's day, nothing had changed (Romans 11:2-6).

(f) God has *judicially blinded* the unbelieving majority to the truth (Romans 11:7-10).

(g) The majority of unbelieving Israel has been *temporarily* set aside to give an opportunity of salvation to the Gentiles, but Gentile salvation is meant to provoke Israel to envy (Romans 11:11).

(h) Israel has paid the price of rejection to give the Gentiles a chance. However, their restoration is assured, and will be **"Life from the dead"** (Romans 11:12-16).

(i) Unbelieving Jews are like olive branches cut off from their own tree. Believing Gentiles are wild live branches grafted in. But Gentiles are not to boast against Jews, because God is able to graft them in again. The Olive Root speaks of the spiritual riches, which flow from God via the Patriarchs, which the Church (composed of Jews and Gentiles) now enjoys, and which unbelieving Israel has temporarily lost (Romans 11:17-24).

(j) A future national repentance is expected for Israel. This is laid before us as a mystery (a secret which can now be revealed Romans 11:25-27). Compare Zechariah 12:10, where the prophet also speaks of a national repentance towards a Messiah, who is also God.

(k) Israel, even in its unbelief, is chosen and loved by God (Romans 11:28).

(l) "As concerning the gospel, they are enemies for **your sakes**" (i.e, You Gentiles) (Romans 11:28). This alone should bring about great thankfulness and love towards the Jews from Gentile Christians.

(m) **"The gifts and calling of God are irrevocable"** (Romans 11:29). This is firm ground on which to believe that God has not rejected Israel.

(n) Paul still identifies himself as a Jew, after becoming a Christian (Acts 21:39).

(o) The NT epistle addressed to the "Hebrews" is a warning to Jewish believers not to return to Judaism as a religious hope, but it clearly still sees these believers as Jewish.

6. The Teaching of Jesus:

(a) Our Lord Jesus does not teach the permanent rejection of Israel. In the parable of the Tenants of the Vineyard in Matthew 21:33-44, He says: "The kingdom of God shall be taken from you, and given to a nation bringing forth the fruits thereof." This is a threat, *not to the Jewish people as such, but to their leaders,* specifically the chief priests and Pharisees (see verse 45).

(b) Jesus foresees a time when the religious Jewish inhabitants of Jerusalem *will* accept Him as Messiah, and this will precede His return (Matthew 23:37-39).

(c) Jesus promises the apostles *they will rule the 12 tribes of Israel* (Matthew 19:28; Luke 22:30).

(d) Our Lord's first mission was to Israel rather than to the Gentiles (Matthew 10:5-6).

7. *The promises of God to the Jews:*
God solemnly promised a land to Abraham (Genesis 15:18-21). This promise is reiterated in sevenfold affirmation in Psalm 105:8-10. Reading this passage carefully, it is impossible to escape the literal meaning for Israel, and instead to apply it metaphorically to the Church. Indeed, if such violence could be done to clear statements of God, then the apparent promises in the NT to the Church would be capable of reinterpretation, and of reapplication to some new people. (Why not to the Moslems, who claim to have replaced the Church?)

Looking closer at this psalm, it says "He hath remembered His **covenant** for ever... which covenant He made with Abraham; and His **oath** unto Isaac; and confirmed the same unto Jacob for a **law,** and to Israel for an **everlasting covenant:** saying, Unto thee will I give the land of Canaan, the lot of your inheritance." These words, "covenant," "oath," "law," "everlasting covenant," if they have any meaning, must surely show the clear will of God, that

Israel should possess the land of Canaan.

8. *God's plan for Israel:*

(a) God's purpose for Israel has always depended on His initiative and election, but Israel's enjoyment of God's blessings has depended on their response as a righteous nation (Deuteronomy 7). Israel is promised abundant blessing when living in a right relationship with God (Leviticus 26:1-13; Deuteronomy 28:1-14), but God promised discipline *(not rejection)* when the nation rebelled (Leviticus 26:14-46; Deuteronomy 28:15-68). Scattering among the nations was the ultimate disciplinary measure, with the promise of regathering ultimately to fulfil His purpose (Deuteronomy 30).

(b) God promised David a royal dynasty reaching eternal dimensions in Israel's Messiah (2 Samuel 7:11-17; 1 Chronicles 17:10-15). Matthew demonstrates that Jesus is that Messiah (Matthew 1:1-16). The angel Gabriel tells Mary that her Son will "reign over the house of Jacob for ever" (Luke 1:33). The name "Jacob" can hardly apply to the Church. Right now, He, Jesus, is still related to Judah, and to David (Revelation 5:5; 22:16).

The Last Lap

(c) When God promised a New Covenant to "the house of Israel" and "the house of Judah" (Jeremiah 31:31), He promised that there would come a day when the Jews should "**all** know me, from the least of them unto the greatest of them" (verse 34). Since such a blessing has never occurred in Israel's history, *this event is yet to come.*

(d) In Ezekiel 36 "the Lord Jehovah" declares "I will (do it)" 22 times concerning Israel's restoration, both to her land, and to her Saviour. Here are some of the things He will do:

i. He will judge the nations for ill-treating Israel (36:3-7).

ii. He will regather Israel to their promised land (verses 8-15).

iii. He will judge Israel for shedding blood in the land, for preferring idols, and for profaning God's name among the nations (verses 16-21).

iv. He will make Israel righteous for the sake of His holy name, not for Israel's sake (verse 22).

v. As a result of Israel's salvation, God will demonstrate to the nations that He is Jehovah (verses 23-28).

vi. When all this has occurred, Israel will know rich spiritual and material blessings (verses 29-38), which Paul describes as "life from the dead" (Romans 11:15).

(e) God has no plan to replace Israel:

- Jeremiah 31:37: "**If** heaven above can be measured, and the foundations of the earth searched out beneath, I will also cast off all the seed of Israel **for all that they have done.**"

- Jeremiah 32:37-41: "I will gather them out of all countries, whither I have driven them in mine anger... and I will bring them again unto this place.... They shall be my people, and I will be their God.... I will give them one heart, and one way, that they may fear me for ever.... I will make an everlasting covenant with them, that I will not turn away from them, to do them good.... I will plant them in this land assuredly **with my whole heart and with my whole soul.**" Such a promise was not fulfilled when a small number of exiles returned from Babylon under Ezra.

- Jeremiah 33:24-26: God quotes what His enemies were saying: "The two families [i.e., Israel and Judah] He hath even cast them off." Then He declares: "**If** my covenant be not with day and night, and if I have not appointed the ordinances of heaven and earth; **then** will I cast away the seed of Jacob, and David my servant."

  Surely, if words bear any meaning at all, and God does not speak, like the Delphic Oracle, in indecipherable riddles, *these promises must guarantee a spiritual and territorial future for the Jews.*

(f) The Church will not be complete before the salvation of Israel:

Romans 11 speaks of Israel's "fulness" (verse 12), *and* "the fulness of the Gentiles" (verse 25). The Greek word in both cases is *pleroma.* The implication is clear: just as Israel provided the foundation members, and the apostolic band which founded the Church, so Israel will be the "fulness" of the Church, the topstone to the whole structure. The national salvation of Israel will involve the great bulk of the Jewish people returning from their apostasy to their own Redeemer, Jesus the Son of God, and God the Son. Israel will thus find her rightful place as part and parcel of the ecclesia of which Jesus spoke in Matthew 16:18. *This event will mean a lot of uncomfortable reconsideration for Gentile Christian theologians as well as for Rabbis!*

9. The promises of God to His Church
Let us now consider only two of the promises made to the Church:

Matthew 16:18: "Upon this rock I will build my church, and the gates of hell shall not prevail against it."

Ephesians 1:11-14:

"In [Him] we have obtained an inheritance, being predestinated according to the purpose of Him who worketh all things after the counsel of His own will: that we should be to the praise of His glory, who first trusted in [Messiah]. In whom ye also trusted, after that ye heard the word of truth, the gospel of your salvation: in whom also after that ye believed, ye were sealed with that Holy Spirit of promise, which is the earnest of our inheritance until the redemption of the purchased possession, unto the praise of His glory."

If the clearly worded promises to Israel can be transferred, then how can we Christians be sure that the promises given to us (as above) shall not be transferred to some other people? God's faithfulness to Israel's promises is the measure of His constancy to us, His Church. The Church is "grafted in" to Israel's olive tree. Her members are citizens of "the commonwealth of Israel" (Ephesians 2:12). How can we then doubt the equally specific promises of grace and election to Israel? If we do, we undermine the foundation of the Church itself.

Church History and Israel

It is sadly true that very soon after the death of the (Jewish) apostles, the Church began to hate and oppose the Jews. Many of the Church Fathers were rabidly anti-Jewish, as was Martin Luther, the great Reformer, in his latter years. However, many godly men have affirmed God's continued purposes for Israel, men such as Bengel, the Wesley brothers, Horatius Bonar, Dr. J. C. Ryle, Charles Spurgeon, and Dr. Martyn Lloyd Jones, to name but a few.

Conclusion

The whole dealing of God with Israel has been mysterious. Indeed, His purpose with the Church was mysterious also. It was not fully understood before the first century AD, as Paul says in Ephesians 3:2-6.

If Israel's leaders had not rejected Jesus, Jesus would not have died; but then there would have been no atonement, or resurrection, and therefore no salvation, either for Jew or Gentile!! Both the blindness of Israel, and the corruption of Pilate were necessary to bring about God's redemption of the Human race.

In the light of what has been set forth in these pages, should we be amazed that our sovereign God has decreed the re-establishment of the territorial State of Israel, or that today there are so many congregations of "Messianic Jews," or Jews believing in Jesus?

Both the State of Israel, and the calling out of Jewish assemblies are clear signs to believers that God's purposes are being worked out, and that exciting, though difficult, times are in view for both the Church and Israel. Surely we should begin to lift up our heads, for our redemption draweth nigh!

THE AUTHOR The Rev. J. Keith Parker, MA (Cantab), BA (Keele)

Brought up in the Church of England, Keith was converted in 1954, studied English and Philosophy at Keele, and Theology at Cambridge.

The Last Lap

He served 11 years as a Methodist Minister, and in 1970 began an 18 year pastorate of an Evangelical church in York. He now exercises a trans-local ministry of teaching and preaching.

Keith is a gifted and well-qualified Bible teacher, available to teach on all aspects of Christian doctrine and experience, as well as on the subject of Israel.

The above article is reprinted by permission of:

Prayer for Israel
P.O. Box 328
Bromley, Kent
United Kingdom
(A ministry focusing on Messianic Fellowships in Israel. Write for an information pack.)

Appendix B

Prophecies from the Approved Jewish Scriptures

All Scripture quotations below are from *The Holy Scriptures*, carefully translated after the best Jewish authorities by Isaac Leeser, New York: Hebrew Publishing Company.

Behold, my servant shall be prosperous, he shall be exalted and extolled, and be placed very high.

Just as many were astonished at thee, so greatly was his countenance marred more than any (other) man's, and his form more than (that of) the sons of men,—

Thus will he cause many nations to jump up in

(astonishment); at him will kings shut their mouth; for what had not been told unto them shall they see, and what they had never heard shall they understand.

Who would have believed our report? and the arm of the Lord—over whom hath it been revealed?

Yea, he grew up like a small shoot before him, and as a root out of a dry land: he had no form nor comeliness, so that we should look at him; and no countenance, so that we should desire him.

He was despised and shunned by men; a man of pains, and acquainted with disease; and as one who hid his face from us was he despised, and we esteemed him not.

But only our diseases did he bear himself, and our pains he carried: while we indeed esteemed him stricken, smitten of God, and afflicted.

Yet he was wounded for our transgressions, he was bruised for our iniquities: the chastisement for our peace was upon him; and through his bruises was healing granted to us.

We all like sheep went astray; every one to his own way did we turn; and the Lord let befall him the guilt of us all.

He was oppressed, and he was also taunted, yet he opened not his mouth; like the lamb which is led to the slaughter, and like a ewe before her shearers is dumb; and he opened not his mouth.

Through oppression and through judicial punishment was he taken away; but his generation—who could tell, that he was cut away out of the land of life, (that) for the transgressions of my people the plague was laid on him?

And he let his grave be made with the wicked, and with the (godless) rich at his death; although he had done no violence, and there was no deceit in his mouth.

But the Lord was pleased to crush him through disease: when (now) his soul hath brought the trespass-offering, then shall he see (his) seed, live many days, and the pleasure of the Lord shall prosper in his hand.

(Freed) from the trouble of his soul shall he see (the good) and be satisfied: through his knowledge shall my righteous servant bring the many to righteousness, while he will bear their iniquities.

Therefore will I divide him (a portion) with the many, and with the strong shall he divide the spoil; because he poured out his soul unto death, and with transgressors was he numbered: while he bore the sin of many, and for the transgressors he let (evil) befall him (Isaiah 52:13-15, 53:1-12).

Behold, days are coming, saith the Lord, when I will make with the house of Israel, and with the house of Judah, a new covenant;

Not like the covenant that I made with their fathers on the day that I took hold of them by the hand to bring them out of the land of Egypt; which my covenant they have broken, although I was become their husband, saith the Lord;

But this is the covenant that I will make with the house of Israel, after those days, saith the Lord, I place my law in their inward parts, and upon their heart will I write it; and I will be unto them for a God, and they shall be unto me for a people.

And they shall not teach any more every man his neighbor, and every man his brother, saying, Know the Lord; for they all shall know me, from the least of them even unto their greatest, saith the Lord; for I will forgive their iniquity, and their sin will I not remember any more (Jeremiah 31:30-33, vs. 31-34 in KJV).

But thou, Beth-lechem Ephratah, the least (though) thou be among the thousands of Judah, (yet) out of thee shall he come forth unto me that is to be ruler in Israel, whose origin is from olden times, from most ancient days (Micah 5:1, v. 2 in KJV).

For thou wilt not abandon my soul to the grave: thou wilt not suffer thy pious (servant) to see corruption (Psalm 16:10).

And after the sixty and two weeks will an anointed one [Messiah] be cut off without a successor to follow him: and the city and the sanctuary will the people of the prince that is coming destroy; but his end will come in a violent overthrow; but until the end of the war devastations are decreed (against it) (Daniel 9:26).

And it shall happen on that day, that (he of) the root of Jesse, who shall stand as an ensign of the people, to him shall nations (come to) inquire: and his resting-place shall be glorious (Isaiah 11:10).

Would you like to have intimacy with God? Say this prayer out loud to God. He will hear you and your name will be written in the Book of Life:

Dear God of Abraham, Isaac, and Jacob, I have committed many sins for which I am sorry. I believe Yeshua died for my sins. And by His stripes my sins are forgiven. You remember my sins no more. Give me the power in Yeshua's name to overcome these sins. I believe Your blood and name break all

curses against me going back up to four generations. Now that I am clean, I make Yeshua my Lord
and Messiah. Yeshua, enter me now and fill me with
the Spirit of God. Amen.

If you said that prayer and meant it, start reading
the Bible every day and begin talking to God (prayer).
Tell Him your problems. When you pray to Him in
Yeshua's name, He will begin to move on your behalf.
Then write or e-mail me at the address at the end of
the book and I will tell you what to do next.

Books available from Messianic Vision

Time Is Running Short by Sid Roth   **$10**
This book will help Christians to understand God's end-time plan for the Jew, the church, and Israel as it is prophetically presented in the book of Esther. It will teach you how to share Yeshua with Jewish people. (220 pages)

There Must Be Something More! by Sid Roth **$10**
Sid Roth thought a million dollars and occult powers could bring happiness. After nearly losing his mind and his marriage, and a close call with suicide, he learned that there *is* something more! Because it is not written in a "preachy" way, this book is an effective tool to reach your Jewish friend or someone trapped in the New Age. It includes a section that answers Jewish objections to Yeshua. (203 pages)

They Thought for Themselves by Sid Roth   **$10**
God told Sid in a dream, "This book will reach more Jewish people with the Gospel than anything you have ever done!" Ten Jewish people share their testimony of breaking with tradition to find their destiny—a destiny built on Yeshua, the sure foundation. They include a former guru, a holocaust survivor, and a Ph.D. (236 pages)

Our Hands Are Stained With Blood
by Dr. Michael Brown   **$12**
Dr. Brown chronicles the sad history of anti-Semitism in the church in one of the most important books we

have ever offered. It will help you to feel God's compassion for the Jewish people. (241 pages)

A Family Guide to the Biblical Holidays
by Robin Scarlata Sampson & Linda Pierce   **$35**
Written by two home-schooling moms, this book is devoted to helping you teach your family (or Bible study class) how God's festival celebrations were a beautiful foreshadow of Jesus the Messiah! Packed with illustrations and activities, the book explains the Messianic significance of the feasts, how they were celebrated in Bible times and how they are observed by Jewish people today. A wonderful tool! (582 pages)

Also, write for our free newsletter and catalog:

Messianic Vision
P.O. Box 1918
Brunswick, GA 31521-1918

(912) 265-2500
(912) 265-3735 fax

e-mail: info@sidroth.org

See our television program and hear our radio show 24 hours a day at www.sidroth.org